Once vegetables were cheap. Now they are expensive and likely to remain so. It is a situation we can accept, or seek to change, for we can do a great deal to ease the burden by growing vegetables ourselves.

Growing one's own vegetables does save money, but there is a lot more to it than that: there is the thrill of having something to show for one's labours, and, best of all, working in a vegetable plot offers a pleasant escape from the office desk, factory bench or from being cooped up indoors all week.

So, even though the money saving is important, it is only half the story. Imagine the joy of crisp little lettuces, crunchy carrots, perfect peas so sweet and tasty, golden onions and ripe red outdoor tomatoes. Vegetables are not the sort of things which should always be hidden at the end of the garden. Is there a more handsome plant than the broad bean with its silvery-green foliage and black and white flowers? Think, too, of the fine, ferny foliage of the carrot or the beetroot with its rich purple leaves.

As well as being decorative, economical and fun to grow, your vegetables will inevitably be of better quality—if only because they are fresher. Commercial growers have to choose varieties tolerant to travelling, disease and mechanical cropping. Your home-grown vegetables will taste better and cost less than any you could buy.

A handsome example of a well thought-out, productive vegetable plot which accommodates both basics, such as beans, carrots, beet and various types of lettuce, as well as the more unusual seakale beet.

3

Basic Vegetable Gardening

by Max Davidson

Marshall Cavendish London & New York

CONTENTS

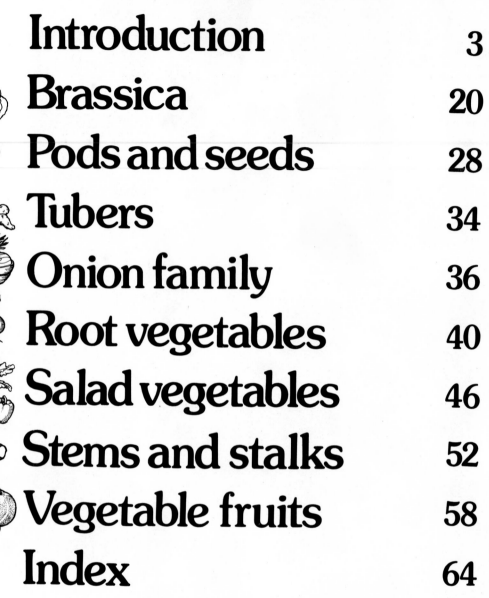

Designer Barbara Howes
Editor Renny Harrop
Illustrator Barbara Howes

Published by Marshall Cavendish Publications Limited
58 Old Compton Street
London W1V 5PA

© Marshall Cavendish Limited 1977

Printed in Great Britain by Redwood Burn Limited

ISBN 0 85685 254 6

Basic Tools

A basic set of good-quality hand tools is essential to establish and maintain a vegetable plot, whatever its size. Buy the best quality you can and take care of them, because they will be in constant use. Cheap tools are a false economy, because they will not last, nor will they be so efficient.

Spade Once you have decided to grow vegetables, there is a certain amount of 'spadework' to be done. And what better way to start than with the spade, the basic tool which you will require to dig over your plot. Digging is not everyone's favourite pastime, so it is worth while spending a bit of money to get the sort of spade you are happy to handle. One with a stainless steel blade may be expensive, but if you have sticky clay soil, it will be an absolute boon in making light work of a heavy task.

Fork You will also require a digging fork, which on previously cultivated or heavy land can fulfil many of the functions of the spade, without the need for the same physical effort. A fork is also necessary for lifting crops such as potatoes.

Rake A rake with a well-made steel head is invaluable for levelling and for breaking down soil to a fine crumbly texture so that seeds can be sown in it. The back of the rake head can also be used to make the shallow impression on the soil surface for seed sowing.

Hoe You will need a hoe to keep down weeds and to stir the top of the soil to prevent it forming a crust, which stops the free passage of moisture and air to the roots of the plants. There are several types of hoe, but the best for general use is the kind with a flat blade called a Dutch hoe. A second type of hoe, which is most useful for close work among plants, thinning seedlings and removing weeds, is the short-handled onion hoe with a swan neck.

Trowel A trowel is the tool one uses when transplanting seedlings. Often such an implement comes as part of a set with a matching hand fork. Like the onion hoe, the hand fork is very useful for those 'close quarters' weeding tasks, where it would be difficult to use the standard Dutch hoe.

Watering can and garden hose Plants require water if they are to make satisfactory growth, and sadly we cannot rely purely on natural rainfall. So your next piece of equipment should be a large watering can, preferably with a choice of roses: a fine rose for watering seedlings and a coarse one for general work. If you have a lot of vegetables to water, you may also need a hose with some sort of sprinkling attachment.

Pressure sprayer Finally, you will require a pressure sprayer to protect your various crops from the insects and diseases which, if allowed to go unheeded, can wipe out all your hard work. The type you choose will again be dictated by the number of vegetables that you grow and, consequently, the spraying you have to do.

Specialist tools

As well as the more fundamental tools there are also a number of implements for special uses, which may be better borrowed or hired.

In many towns nowadays, there are tool hire shops. So if you are new to gardening, you could always hire those items which you think you are likely to need least often. Hire shops too can let you rent the kind of equipment which you may not normally think of buying, a mechanical cultivator for instance. Such a machine will make light work of the average vegetable plot and save you many hours of labour. It is also marvellous for breaking up the hard soil of a new garden with ease and efficiency.

Optional extras Just as with a car one can get from Point A to Point B satisfactorily with the basic model, similarly in the garden, but a few of the optional extras can make a world of difference to the getting there. Among my optional extras I would number cloches, cold frames, and a greenhouse. A garden shed could also be useful for the storage of tools, composts and fertilisers when the garage is already fully occupied by car, bicycles and toys.

Cloches Cloches provide an excellent way of giving protection to tender vegetables. They also enable seeds to be sown earlier, improve crop yields and make possible the successful cultivation of vegetables in areas where without protection they would fail. The cheapest type of cloche is the continuous polythene tunnel which can be used to cover things like lettuces or early root crops. The cloche as well as giving protection from the elements also shields the crop from the attention of hungry birds. Glass cloches are said to give better growing

Opposite page *A set of good-quality hand tools is essential to establish and maintain a vegetable plot, whatever its size. The basic tools with which most of the work will be carried out are the spade, fork, hoe, rake and trowel.*

1 A tool-shed is useful but not essential. Do not site it on valuable growing space, and make sure there is easy access via a path between shed and plot. Minimum useful size for a tool-shed is about 1 x 1.2m (3x4ft).

2 A greenhouse will prove a valuable addition to any garden large enough to take one. It needs to be situated where there is plenty of sunlight. A conventional greenhouse with an apex roof should be erected on a north-south line. Lean-to structures should be placed against a sunny wall.

3 and 4 Most gardens have sufficient room to incorporate a frame. They function like a miniature cold greenhouse and are ideal for raising early vegetables from seed. They should be positioned so that the sun reaches them.

5 A cloche is a glass, or plastic, tent- or tunnel-shaped enclosure, designed to protect crops during harsh weather conditions. As well as providing a shield from the elements a cloche will also help protect crops from birds.

conditions because they allow more light to reach the plants. However, they are fairly expensive and easily broken. For this reason I prefer the modern rigid plastic cloches, which are large enough to cover quite tall plants and which give many years of useful service for a comparatively modest outlay.

Glass frames Glass does come into its own with a garden frame. Such frames can be thought of as miniature cold greenhouses and they soon pay for themselves by enabling you to raise early vegetable plants from seed, such as cauliflowers and cabbages. They can also be used in cold districts for growing lettuces during winter, and they provide a summer home for cucumbers and courgettes. Frames can be obtained with glass all round or with wooden sides and glass lights. The former type is best in mild areas; the latter is the better bet in cold districts where the wood helps to retain warmth and offers more protection from chilling winds.

Greenhouses The ultimate in the use of glass in the garden is the greenhouse. There are so many kinds that one simply has to make up one's mind as to the type that is most suitable on cost and aesthetic grounds. Wood has become very expensive, but some of the modern aluminium houses are excellent value for money as well as looking most attractive. A word of warning—if you live by the seaside and buy an aluminium glass-house, make sure that its frame has been treated with plastic, as sea air is corrosive on aluminium.

Whatever size greenhouse you choose, you will soon wish that it were larger. So, within reason, get the biggest you can afford. A greenhouse 2.4m by 2.4m (8ft by 8ft) is ideal for the average garden. Even without any form of heating it will enable you to grow tomatoes and cucumbers, and you will be able to raise all kinds of vegetable plants from seed. However, with heat, you could widen your field of interest to include things like aubergines and capsicums and to grow many vegetables out of season. Heat can be provided by paraffin, electricity or gas. Compact gas heaters, fuelled by bottled butane, are efficient, have about the cheapest running costs, and the carbon dioxide produced as a by-product helps the growth of the plants.

Clearing and preparing the site
Before you can consider any refinements in vegetable growing, it is necessary to concentrate on the basics. Namely

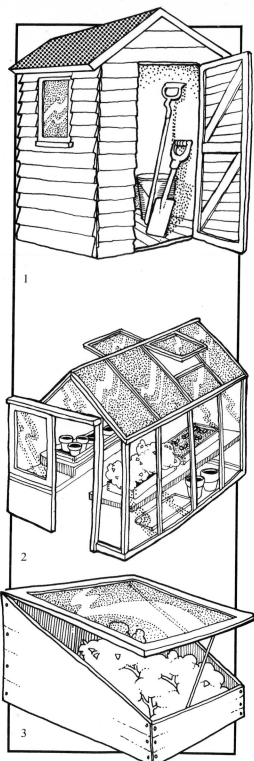

preparing the vegetable plot itself. Ideally, this should be in a position which gets plenty of sunshine and is away from overhanging trees although these can be improved by pruning.

Removal of turf and weeds
If you are starting from scratch, with a garden which has never been previously cultivated, your first problem could be the removal of turf or a mass of weeds. When the turf is simply of the meadow type, it can be skimmed off in strips 5cm (2in) thick and stacked in a corner where

4

5

be eradicated by using a brushwood killer. As both of these weedkillers persist in the soil for about three months, they are best applied in late summer or early autumn in order to enable you to grow vegetables the following year.

Where the uncultivated soil is a mass of weeds of all types, the method which I have found most successful in the past is to treat the ground with a weedkiller containing paraquat and diquat. Such a weedkiller burns off all the top growth and yet is inactivated on contact with the soil. Most weeds will be killed with the initial treatment. The dead foliage can then be raked up and burned. After two or three weeks the regrowth of persistent weeds can be killed with a second treatment. These weedkillers are, however, extremely poisonous. If you have children or animals around it is preferable to fork out carefully all the roots of those perennial gardening horrors such as dandelions and bindweed and burn them.

Digging over

Having dealt with the weeds, the next task is to dig over the soil. Provided there is no 'hard pan' under the surface, it will be sufficient to dig over the soil in the normal way. However, if the soil is stony, or there is an impervious layer of compacted soil and stones—'hard pan'—just below the surface, special treatment is called for. In this case you should fork over the soil to about twice the depth of the fork and leave the soil rough so that it is exposed to the effects of rain and frost.

The best time to dig heavy soils is in autumn or early winter. Never dig clay soils when they are wet and sticky; you will only make matters worse. Light soils, which do not need weathering, can be dug at any time.

Improving the soil

The texture of soil, be it crumbly, sandy or clayey, can be partially determined or altered by the addition of organic matter. Such organic matter breaks down in the soil to form humus, a dark substance which is the life blood of soil. Humus enables the soil to absorb air and moisture and it ensures that plants can form healthy root systems. Without humus, the benefits of chemical fertilisers are largely wasted.

Manure and compost

There are several ways in which the soil can be supplied with organic matter. The first is by digging in farmyard manure. Much better in my opinion is to use your own garden compost, made in a properly

it will rot down to provide useful compost or lawn top dressing at a later date. The trick to getting the turfs to rot down satisfactorily is to stack them in alternate layers, grass side to grass side, with a sprinkling of sulphate of ammonia between the layers to help the rotting process, although this is not essential.

If the uncultivated land contains rough weed grasses such as the one called couch, you are best advised to treat the area first with a selective weedkiller such as Dalapon. Really tough woody weeds, such as brambles and ivy, can successfully

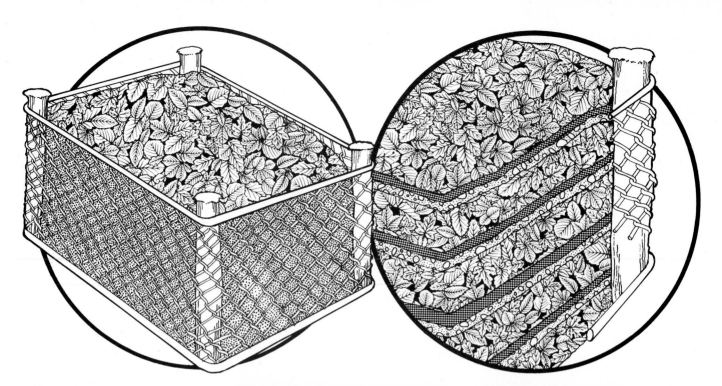

Above *One of the best ways of supplying the soil in your garden with organic matter is by making and using garden compost.*
1 The ideal method is to buy either one, or preferably two, wire or plastic compost bins or to make them yourself. Each compost heap needs a space of about one square metre (yard). They should be positioned where they are easy to reach. All organic matter, including kitchen waste, can go on the heap, but not weeds and diseased plants which should be destroyed.
2 Build up the heap in layers and sandwich with a compost activator. Leave for six months for the material to break down.

Right *The colour of a soil is often an indication of its type.*
1 Loamy sand.
2 One of the many types of clay.
3 A well-balanced loam.
4 A sandy clay loam.

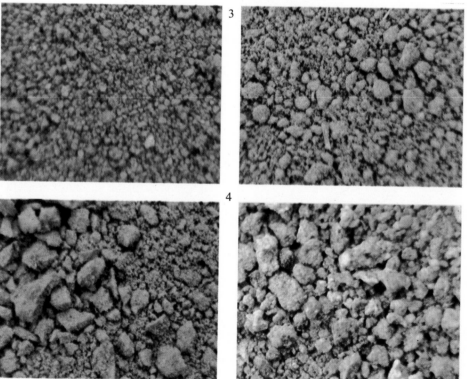

constructed compost heap. For most gardens the best plan is to buy a couple of wire or plastic compost bins. Alternatively, you could make them from plastic fencing netting and stout posts. The minimum size should be one cubic metre (one cubic yard). All organic matter including kitchen waste can go on the heap with the exception of perennial weeds, diseased plants and rose prunings which should be burned. The technique of producing good compost is to build up the heap in layers of well-mixed material like a sponge cake. Each 23cm (9in)

layer should be sprinkled with a compost activator. There is no need to disturb the heap until it is ready for use in around six months. Because of the time it takes to produce compost and the fact that most organic matter is available during the growing season — grass cuttings, for instance—two heaps are the minimum for satisfactory results.

If your garden is new, it is unlikely that you will have sufficient organic material to make compost. For a small area you can use peat as a substitute to improve the texture of the soil.

Green manuring There is also a technique called 'green manuring', that is growing your own manure on the soil to be fed. Seeds of a fast growing plant such as mustard are broadcast over the soil in early summer and dug into the soil just before the plants start to flower. Sulphate of ammonia should be scattered over at the rate of 28g per sq m (1oz per sq yd) to speed the rotting process, although this is not essential.

Soil type and testing
Animal manure and garden compost not only improve the physical structure of the soil but provide sufficient plant foods for both vegetables and fruit. Peat contains little plant food at all. Many gardeners make use of garden chemicals. Before considering giving the soil any chemical treatment, it is wise to buy an inexpensive soil test kit to check the soil for acidity and alkalinity.

Applying the information Calcium, which is added to the soil in the form of lime, controls the acidity or alkalinity of the soil. Certain vegetables have a marked preference for the correct soil acidity, and providing the ideal conditions also helps

to discourage disease. The best time to apply lime is during autumn or winter.

The other plant foods can be supplied by straight fertilisers; nitro chalk as the source of nitrogen for instance. But it is generally most convenient to use a compound granular vegetable fertiliser. For many years gardeners relied on a standard formula with the name National Growmore. Nowadays the fertiliser firms have found ways of improving vegetable crops by varying the proportions of the ingredients. If you have made a soil test, you should be able to choose the fertiliser which comes closest to matching the requirements of the soil in your particular garden.

Fertilizers
General fertilisers are usually applied a week or two before seed sowing or planting out. Certain crops which require supplementary feeding are given either additional dressings of general fertiliser or a specific straight fertiliser to provide the food, possibly nitrogen, during the growth of the plants. Normally you will find all you need to know about how much to use and when to apply on the back of the fertiliser bag.

Below *Certain vegetables require supplementary feeding and need to be given additional dressings of either a general, or a specific fertiliser to provide food, such as nitrogen, during the growth of the plant.*
1 Nitrogenous fertiliser is applied around the neck of an onion.
2 The soil is scraped over with a cultivator to work in the fertiliser.

Year One

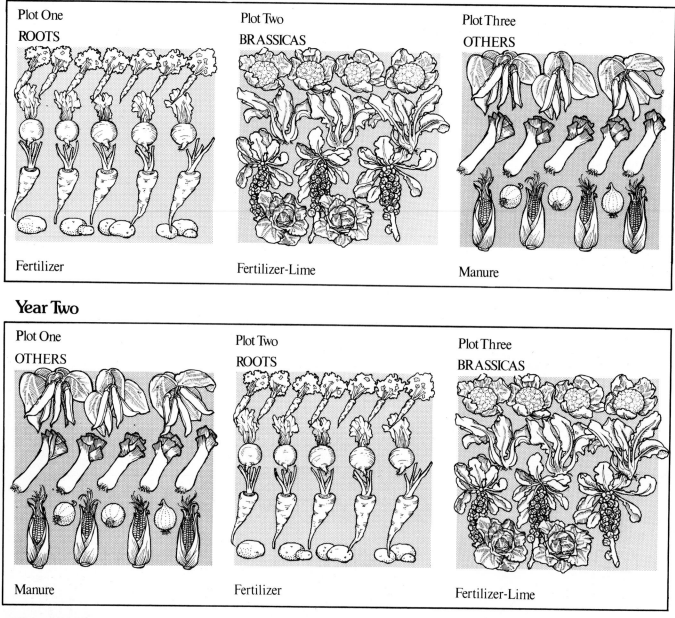

Plot One
ROOTS

Fertilizer

Plot Two
BRASSICAS

Fertilizer-Lime

Plot Three
OTHERS

Manure

Year Two

Plot One
OTHERS

Manure

Plot Two
ROOTS

Fertilizer

Plot Three
BRASSICAS

Fertilizer-Lime

Year Three

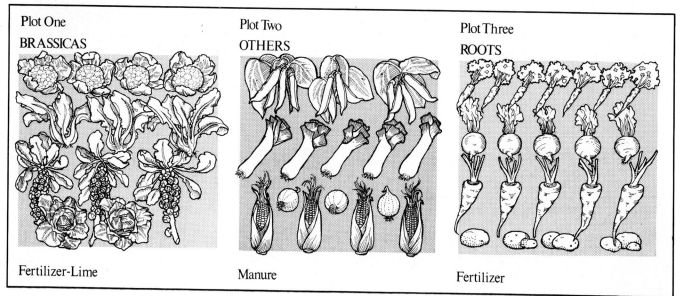

Plot One
BRASSICAS

Fertilizer-Lime

Plot Two
OTHERS

Manure

Plot Three
ROOTS

Fertilizer

Crop rotation

Fertilisers are expensive and over-use can soon dissipate any saving you may make in growing your own vegetables, moreover, certain plants differ in the amounts of fertiliser and soil treatment they require. In order to keep the condition of the soil in balance and to avoid the risk of disease, such as club root, we have to practise crop rotation, which simply means that no crop should be grown on the same piece of land two years running.

Let us assume that you have one vegetable plot. The simplest method of establishing a rotation system is to divide the ground into three approximately equal sections. The first year Plot One can be used for root crops such as beetroot, carrots, potatoes, swedes and parsnips. For such crops a general fertiliser may be applied before sowing. In Plot Two you should grow the brassicas — Brussels sprouts, broccoli, cabbages, cauliflowers and spinach. For these crops the soil should be enriched with compost, limed if necessary in winter—make a soil test. This plot may be dressed with granular fertiliser before sowing. Plot Three should be used to accommodate all the other vegetables which do not fit into the categories of roots or brassicas. So, in Plot Three, you could grow others such as beans, celery, cucumbers, endives, leeks, lettuces, marrows, onions, peas, radishes, sweet corn and tomatoes. The soil for these vegetables should be enriched with compost in winter and may be dressed with general fertiliser before sowing or planting.

So in Year One you have in your plot three sections: roots, brassicas and others. In Year Two the arrangement becomes others, roots and brassicas. In Year Three it is brassicas, others and roots. By Year Four the cycle is complete and you are back where you started.

This situation is the ideal one. In many small vegetable plots proper rotation is impossible, but by careful planning, from year to year, you should be able to avoid growing the same vegetable in the same spot two years running.

Intercropping Some vegetables mature quickly; others can take months before they are ready for harvesting. So that we can get the maximum productivity out of our gardens, it is a good idea to grow fast-maturing crops between the rows of the slower maturing vegetables. Between the rows of beans (broad, French and runner) you can grow lettuces, radishes and beetroots. Broad beans can also be intercropped with Brussels sprouts. The brassicas themselves can all be intercropped with lettuce, beetroot and dwarf beans; and between rows of celery you can have peas, dwarf beans and lettuces.

Catch-cropping This involves growing a fast-maturing crop in ground that is empty for only a short period between the harvesting of one crop and the sowing or planting of the next. An example of this method is the sowing of carrots (in

Opposite page *The purpose of crop rotation is two-fold. In the first place, to get the best possible return from the soil, and in the second, to keep certain devastating pests and diseases in check. The principle, as illustrated in this diagram, is very simple to follow so long as you remember that the three plots must be the same size, and that perennial vegetables, such as globe artichokes and asparagus, which have to stay in one place, are excluded.*

Below *Two ways of getting extra use are by catch-cropping and inter-cropping. In 1, lettuces have been planted on the ridges of celery trenches, and in 2, lettuces have been intercropped between rows of runner beans.*

1

2

11

early spring) on ground which will later be planted with cabbages (in mid to late spring). Radishes are a very good 'catch crop' as they mature within six or seven weeks from sowing. Accurate timing is vital as if you sow your catch crop too late, it won't have matured before the time when you must plant the main crop in the same row.

Yield

Few people nowadays have gardens big enough to grow a really wide selection of vegetables, but with careful planning it is marvellous what can be achieved. One of the problems is that there is always the temptation to grow too much of one particular vegetable simply because the seeds are there. Most seeds have a storage life of two years and many will keep in good condition for several years. So only sow to raise the number of plants you are likely to require. For example, 12 cauliflowers, even where a deep freeze is available, should be adequate, especially when one considers that by successional sowings it is possible to harvest cauliflowers at different times of the year. Your family's tastes will also govern what

you do and do not grow. Some vegetables too give a greater productivity for the same space than others. For instance a row of runner beans will provide 18kg (40lb) to a 3m (10ft) row while a similar row of peas will only yield 2kg (4lb). Choosing the right varieties of vegetable seed is also important. It is worthwhile paying a bit more for some of the F1 hybrids when the end result is better crops and tastier vegetables. Take calabrese (Italian sprouting broccoli), for example. Green Comet F1 Hybrid is noteworthy for exceptional earliness and large heads. Then there is the cabbage. Most cabbages grow too large for small gardens, but with a variety like Hispi F1 Hybrid you can have superb cabbages with no waste that need be spaced just 38cm (15in) apart with 25cm (10in) between the rows.

Even the humble lettuce can be much more useful if you choose the best possible varieties for your situation. Tom Thumb enables you to have butterhead lettuces that can be grown 15cm (6in) apart. If you prefer a cos lettuce, there is Little Gem which needs to be just 10cm (4in) apart.

Opposite page *The best way to store surplus onions for winter use is to plait them with raffia and hang them in a cool, dry place.*

Below *When you first begin to grow vegetables, it is very tempting either to grow too many of one particular vegetable or to grow vegetables that are not popular with the rest of your household. Always try to tailor your planting to your family's needs.*

Above *Freezing is the most effective form of long term storage for vegetables in terms of flavour, texture and colour. Most seed firms give advice in their catalogues on varieties of vegetable most suited to freezing.*

Storing vegetables

Another advantage of growing your own vegetables is that you can store the surplus crop for use during the winter when shop vegetables are at their most expensive. Storing root crops is easy. With crops such as beetroots, carrots, celeriac, parsnips, salsify, swedes and turnips, it is just a matter of cutting off the tops and storing the roots in layers in boxes, with peat separating the individual layers. The boxes themselves should be stored in a dry, frostproof place such as a garden shed or garage.

Onions and shallots are best plaited with raffia and hung in a cool dry place. Alternatively you can hang them in plastic nets strung between garage roof beams.

Marrows and squashes, once the skins have been allowed to dry and harden, will keep for months on slatted shelves in a cool spot.

Freezing The modern way of preserving vegetables is to deep freeze them. Vegetables like beans, peas, broccoli, Brussels sprouts, cauliflower, courgettes, and sweet corn are all splendid for deep freezing. Just think, by freezing your own vegetables you will be able to harvest the entire crop while it is young and tasty. Some varieties of vegetables freeze particularly well without any loss of flavour. Most seed firms give advice in their catalogues on varieties suitable for freezing, but examples are the pea Hurst Green Shaft, the broad bean Masterpiece Green Longpod, the runner bean Enorma, the Brussels sprouts Peer Gynt and the cauliflower All The Year Round.

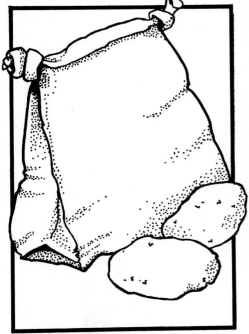

Sowing seeds

The beauty of growing vegetables is that many of the seeds can be sown directly outdoors without fuss. The main problem for most people is to make the seeds germinate. From experience I have found two main reasons for lack of success in getting seeds to germinate. The first is sowing the seeds far too early. The beginning of March may be fine for the South of England, but in the Midlands you are far better to wait until the end of March, while in Scotland sometime in April is early enough. The second reason

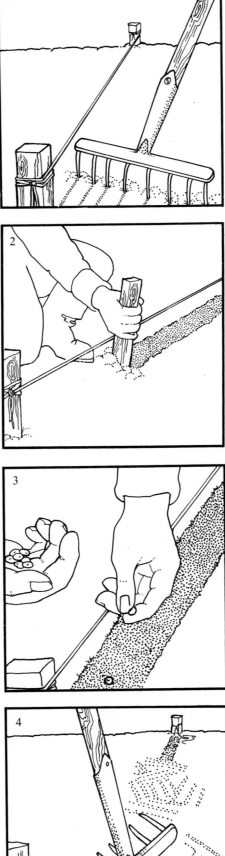

Far left Dark, cool storage is essential for potatoes. Too high a temperature causes sprouting; too low a temperature produces a sweet taste. Store in paper bags in a larder, but never refrigerate them.

Left To sow seeds out of doors:
1   The soil should be worked over lightly with a hoe and then raked gently back and forth until you have produced a fine tilth. Decide on the length of your row and insert a stick into the ground to which a length of string is attached. Run the string along the ground to the required length and tie it to a second stick at the other end so that it is taut. This will help you keep your drill straight.
2   Make a drill, that is a shallow furrow, with either a hoe or wooden stick, such as the handle of a rake, to the required depth and width along the length of string. It should be of uniform depth; most drills are about 1cm ($\frac{1}{2}$in) deep, although for larger seeds, such as peas, they may need to be as much as 5cm (2in) deep.
3   Sow the seeds as thinly as possible to avoid overcrowding and excessive thinning of plants later on.
4   Once you have distributed the seed down the row, cover it by drawing the back of your garden rake along the drill. This tips the ridge of soil along each side of the furrow back into the centre and levels off the soil. Immediately after sowing, water very gently so that you do not disturb the soil. Mark each row with the variety of vegetable and date of sowing.

for failure is sowing the seeds too deeply. Here one has to use a bit of common sense. A depth of 2.5cm (1in) may be all right in fine sandy soil, but in heavier soils the same seeds will be happier just 1cm ($\frac{1}{2}$in) deep.

If you have cloches, you can help your seeds along by placing the cloches over the soil where you intend to sow to warm it slightly and to prevent the soil from becoming excessively wet. With cloches, you could well sow your seeds up to a month earlier than my suggested dates.

Successful germination of the seeds and the ultimate performance of the plants will of course be governed by the amount of initial preparation you give to the soil. We have already covered the importance of adequate cultivation and feeding of the soil, but seeds need even more attention. The soil should be worked over lightly with a hoe and then raked gently back and forth until you have produced a fine tilth. If necessary, work some peat into the top 2-4cm (1-2in) of soil. Do not worry about small stones; they will not be any problem for your seedlings.

It is essential once you have made your drills to sow the seeds as thinly as possible

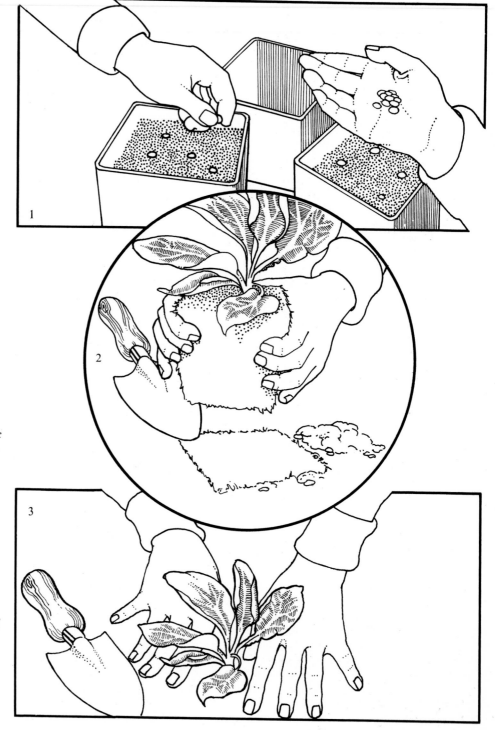

1 To sow seeds indoors, fill plastic pots or seed trays with a suitable peat-based seed compost. Sow the recommended number of seeds in each pot or tray and water the compost thoroughly. Cover with newspaper if necessary, and place in a warm, dark place until they germinate. When the seedlings are large enough to handle, they should be transplanted to larger pots or trays filled with potting compost.
2 When transplanting seedlings, choose a cloudy day or evening, and dig out a hole with a trowel large enough to accommodate the plant and its roots.
3 Put in the plant and firm the soil around the stem with your fingers.

16

so that they do not have to compete with one another and you do not have to do excessive thinning later on. The modern way to cut down on the need to thin is to use pelleted seed: that is, seeds coated with clay, which makes them a convenient size to be placed individually. Pelleted seed is marvellous for things like carrots and lettuces. However there is a trick to getting good germination of this type of seed. Once you have made your seed drills, water the bottom of the drill thoroughly if the soil is on the dry side, so that the clay casings come into contact immediately with moist soil.

Remember to sow with the intention of raising no more than the number of plants which you can use. It is pointless, for example, to produce 30 lettuces which are ready for lifting the same week. Successional sowings at intervals of two to three weeks is the answer.

Thinning and transplanting As soon as the seedlings appear, they will start to compete for food and water, so they should be thinned as soon as practicable. The best idea is to do the job in two stages: first, perhaps, to 5cm (2in) apart and then to their final spacing. Most thinnings have to be discarded but those of onions can be eaten as spring onions with salads and those of lettuce can be transplanted elsewhere. With the brassica crops this process is taken a stage further since the plants are normally raised in a nursery or seed bed and later transplanted to their final quarters, which may, in turn, have been vacated by another, faster-growing, crop. When transplanting, the secret of success is to do the job on a cloudy day or in the evening and digging out a hole with a trowel large enough to accommodate the plant and its roots. Fill the hole with water, allow the water to be absorbed and then put in the plant and firm the soil around its stem with your fingers. Should the weather be dry, the newly transplanted vegetables must be kept well-watered until they are obviously established.

Sowing seeds in containers Not all vegetables unfortunately can be raised from seed outdoors. Some, such as tomatoes, have to be sown indoors and planted outdoors once they have been gradually acclimatized to outdoor living. Such seeds can be sown in plastic pots or seed trays containing a suitable peat-based compost. These new composts really are superb. Their ability to retain water and the way in which they encourage plants to form healthy roots makes raising plants indoors child's play.

After you have sown the seeds in their containers, water the compost thoroughly. Then cover with newspaper and, if necessary, place the containers in a warm, dark cupboard until the seeds germinate. When the seedlings are large enough to handle, they should be transplanted either to 8cm (3in) diameter peat pots or to larger seed trays containing a suitable peat-based potting compost.

The advantage of using the peat pots is that later on the plants can be put directly into the ground in their peat pots, without any further check to their growth. The roots simply grow through the pot sides, and the pots break down to combine with the surrounding soil. Plants in seed trays should be 7.5cm (3in) apart in each direction. It is essential to keep newly transplanted seedlings out of direct sunlight for the first few days.

Some vegetable plants can be raised by sowing the seeds directly into peat pots or peat blocks. This practice is most useful with the brassicas and produces better yields in areas with poor growing conditions. To be successful peat pots have to be kept moist. The best way of doing this is to pack them tightly in plastic containers. A $2\frac{1}{2}$ litre (half gallon) plastic ice cream container, incidentally, will hold four 7.5cm (3in) peat pots comfortably.

General care and maintenance Once you have established your seedlings they need careful nurturing. The first essential is water, either from a watering can or hose. You can also help to retain moisture in the soil by hoeing lightly around the plants and keeping the soil crumbly. It is also useful with some plants to put down a 2.5cm (1in) moisture-retaining *and* weed-suppressing layer, or mulch, of *moist* peat. Weeds themselves can be virtually banished by regular hoeing. It is a good practice too to keep the vegetable garden tidy, to clear up fallen leaves and to dispose of unwanted plants on the compost heap. It also makes the year's work easier if you dig over a piece of the vegetable plot as soon as it is vacated.

Clearing up after harvesting not only makes the garden look better, it also gets rid of rubbish (to the compost heap, of course!) under which slugs may hide and breed.
However, even the most well-managed vegetable plot has its share of problems from time to time, particularly from pests, fungal growth and diseases. Here is a guide to help you recognize your enemies and how to deal with them:

Pests&diseases	Symptoms	Treatment
Aphids (greenfly, blackfly)	Tiny green, yellow or black insects clustered on leaves and stems. Some leaves and stems stunted and discoloured.	Spray with a proprietary insecticide such as malathion, but preferably one which is harmless to man and wildlife. Ladybirds eat aphids.
Botrytis (grey mould)	Leaves and fruit covered with grey fungus. Fruit rots. Plants rot off at soil level. Particularly affects vegetables, fruits and lettuce	Spray with a proprietary fungicide at first sign of attack and repeat according to instructions on the pack. Badly affected plants should be destroyed.
Cabbage root fly	Members of the cabbage family (all the brassicas) wilt and become bluish.	None, but preventive measures should be taken. Plant in well-manured or well-composted soil, and firm well. Dip the roots of seedlings when planting out in mercurous chloride (Calomel dust) or water with Lindex.
Carrot fly	Maggots mine in roots.	None. Preventive measures are to delay sowing until May, to bury all carrot thinnings which are too small for use in the compost heap, and never leave broken carrot foliage around. The carrot fly is attracted by the smell of the leaves, so it is worth planting onions between the rows of carrots to help mask the aroma. A chemical preventive is to treat seeds with Gamma-BHC before sowing.
Caterpillars	Holes eaten out of leaves in spring and summer.	Examine vegetables for caterpillars at intervals. Pick them off and kill them. Spraying with derris (harmless to man and wildlife except fish) is a preventive measure.
Club root	Plants of the cabbage family (brassicas) become stunted. Roots are swollen.	None. Prevent by ensuring that the soil is rich in organic matter (e.g. garden compost); apply lime to soil if necessary to prevent acidic conditions favoured by club root fungus. Dusting planting holes when transplanting with mercurous chloride (Calomel dust) is a chemical preventive measure.
Cut worms and leatherjackets	Plants collapse with stems eaten through at, or below, ground level.	Dust soil with Sevin dust or hoe Gamma-BHC lightly into the soil. Alternatively, remove and kill these pests during cultivation. Hoe regularly to expose the pests to insect-eating birds, frogs and toads. The pests can be 'baited'. Baits are slices of potato or carrot skewered and buried an inch or so in the soil. Remove baits daily and pick off cut worms and leatherjackets.
Damping off	Seedlings collapse at ground level.	Use only sterile seed compost when raising plants in trays and pots. Watering infected seedlings with chestnut compound can prevent the infection from spreading.

Pests&diseases	Symptoms	Treatment
Flea beetles	Small round holes particularly in the leaves of radish, swede, turnip and some other vegetables.	Keep seedlings well-watered in dry weather. Hoe often. Dust leaves when dry with Derris powder.
Leaf miners	Irregular channels or whitish blisters in leaves.	Pinch and crush maggots in leaves; burn tops of badly infested plants when these are dug up. Winter digging exposes pupae to birds. Malathion and nicotine are two chemical controls.
Mice	Beans and peas fail to appear despite adequate precautions.	Bait and set traps beneath cloches. Place Warfarin bait inside pieces of narrow plastic piping.
Onion fly	Whitish maggots in young bulbs.	None; preventive measures are to sow seeds in late summer or early winter, raise onions from 'sets'. Bury unwanted onion thinnings within the compost heap. Take care when thinning and hoeing that onion foliage is not damaged. The odour of damaged foliage attracts egg-laying onion flies. Burn affected plants.
Pea moth	Maggots found in the pods.	None. Prevent by sowing in March and early April. Kelvedon Wonder and Foremost are reputed to be less susceptible to attack. Keep plants well-watered during flowering period. Shallow digging in winter exposes pupae to birds.
Root aphid	Grey mealy pests on roots of lettuce. Plants wilt.	Dig up and burn affected plants. Only when this pest is known to be prevalent should preventive chemical measures, such as watering the soil with liquid Malathion or nicotine, be taken.
Slugs and snails	Leaves chewed. Faint silvery trails around plants.	Keep the plot tidy and free from decaying matter. Search for and kill slugs and snails especially in the late evening with the aid of a torch. Protect plants with metaldehyde pellets.
Wireworm	Yellowish brown thread-like grubs in soil which feed on root crops.	Soil should be dusted with Gamma-BHC. Potatoes and carrots should not be grown until the pest is eliminated as Gamma-BHC will taint the crop. Kill any found during digging and hoeing. Baits (slices of carrot or potato skewered and buried an inch or two in the soil) may be used. Often a serious pest where grassland or lawn is converted into a vegetable garden. Cultivation exposes this pest to birds.
Birds	Leaves or seedlings eaten down to soil level.	Grow seedlings under plastic netting or wire netting guards. Cover green crops with pigeon netting.

Cabbage, winter, spring or summer

The edible head of a cabbage consists of leaves wrapped very tightly around the crown of the plant.

Cabbage, winter, spring or summer

Brassica oleracea Capitata (fam. *Cruciferae*)
Biennial
Size 30cm (1ft) to 60cm (2ft) high, by 30cm (1ft) to 60cm (2ft) wide, depending on chosen variety.
Edible part The leaves.
Climate preferred Cool temperate.
Aspect Open.
Sowing to harvest time Summer and winter varieties 20 to 35 weeks; spring-heading varieties 36-40 weeks.
Yield 1kg to 2kg (2lb to 4lb) a plant.
Soil Ordinary well-drained garden soil, well-consolidated and free from air pockets.

Cabbages are one of the easiest vegetables to grow especially in areas where growing conditions for less hardy vegetables are generally poor. Careful choice should be made of the varieties grown so that maximum use of the available space can be obtained. By planting a combination of spring, summer and winter cabbages in succession, it is possible to eat fresh cabbage throughout the year.

Sowing and planting

As cabbages require well consolidated soil, digging of the plot should be carried out several months in advance of planting. Organic matter should be incorporated when digging and lime can be added if necessary in winter. Should you feel unable to let the plot lie idle, plant your cabbages on soil vacated by a different crop. The seed should be sown thinly in rows 1cm ($\frac{1}{2}$in) deep. Winter varieties: sow outdoors at the end of April or May and transplant during June; spring varieties: sow in July and August and transplant in September or October; summer varieties: sow indoors or under glass in February and plant out at the beginning of April—alternatively sow outdoors in April and transplant in May or June. The seedlings should be transplanted to their final positions when they have six leaves. About two weeks prior to transplanting give the cabbage plot a dressing of 112g per sq m (4oz per sq yd) of granular vegetable fertiliser, if the soil lacks sufficient plant food. When transplanting, firm the soil around the plants and water thoroughly. Allow 30cm to 45cm (1ft to 1$\frac{1}{2}$ft) between the plants each way depending on the variety. Hoe the soil lightly to keep down weeds and water regularly as cabbages grown in drought conditions have a poor flavour.

Pests and diseases

Aphids, caterpillars, club root and root fly.

Harvesting

Cut fresh from the garden as required.

Cabbage, red and savoy

Red cabbages are extremely decorative in the vegetable garden as well as being easy to grow. They are also very tasty casseroled with apples, onions and wine or vinegar, although they are often grown for pickling alone.

Sowing and planting
The soil should be prepared in exactly the same way as for winter, spring and summer cabbages. The seed should be sown 1cm ($\frac{1}{2}$in) deep outdoors at the end of April or in May and the seedlings transplanted to their final positions in June. The crop should be looked after in the same way as other cabbages.

Pests and diseases
Aphids, caterpillars, club root and root fly. If your garden attracts slugs, it is advisable to put a ring of lime around each plant after planting. This not only provides the cabbage with the lime it needs, but also deters the slugs from attacking the stems at surface level.

Harvesting
Cut fresh from the garden as required. Store by pickling.

Savoy cabbages are very easily grown, especially in cold northern areas. A very useful autumn and winter vegetable, they are crisp, and their crinkly leaves and solid hearts make the best coleslaw.

Sowing and planting
Savoys should be sown in the same way as ordinary winter varieties. However, since they make much larger plants, they should be transplanted 60cm (2ft) apart in each direction. Cultivate as other cabbages.

Pests and diseases
As other cabbages.

Harvesting
Cut fresh from the garden as required.

Above left *The red cabbage has a delightful flavour but a limited season.*

Above right *The Savoy cabbage is characterized by its wrinkled, puckered leaves.*

Below *Cabbages should be transplanted with as much soil attached to their roots as possible.*

Cabbage, red
Brassica oleracea Capitata (fam. *Cruciferae*)
Biennial
Size 30cm (1ft) to 60cm (2ft) high. Large or compact round heads depending on variety.
Edible part The leaves.
Climate preferred Cool temperate.
Aspect Open.
Sowing to harvest time 30 to 35 weeks.
Yield 1kg to 2kg (2lb to 4lb) a plant.
Soil Ordinary well-drained garden soil, well consolidated and free from air pockets.

Cabbage, savoy
Brassica oleracea Bullata (fam. *Cruciferae*)
Biennial
Size 60cm (2ft) high; by 60cm (2ft) wide.
Edible part The leaves.
Climate preferred Cool temperate; frost improves flavour.
Aspect Open.
Sowing to harvest time 20 to 35 weeks.
Yield 2kg to 4kg (4lb to 9lb) a plant.
Soil Ordinary well-drained garden soil, well consolidated and free from air pockets.

Brussels sprouts

Brussels sprouts have been developed by careful plant breeding to produce tight, little cabbage-like heads right around the stem. Their flavour is actually improved by a touch of frost.

Brussels sprouts

Brassica oleracea Gemmifera (fam. *Cruciferae*)
Biennial
Size Small hybrid varieties suitable for the garden are little more than 75cm (30in) high.
Edible part The buttons on the stalks and the loose head at the top of the plants.
Climate preferred Cool temperate.
Aspect Open, yet sheltered from strong winds.
Sowing to harvest time 28 to 36 weeks depending on the variety.
Yield 1kg (2lb) of sprouts to a plant.
Soil Firm soil rich in humus.

Brussels sprouts are a valuable green crop for winter months and a rich source of vitamin C. By choosing the right varieties, it is possible to have fresh sprouts throughout the period between October and March.

Sowing and planting

The soil for Brussels sprouts must contain plenty of organic material and should be limed; on no account should it be acid. As with cabbages, the plot should ideally be prepared a few months before it is required for setting out the plants, but most gardeners will have to make do with land occupied previously by an unrelated crop. The seed should be sown thinly outdoors between March and April, depending on the variety and location, 1cm ($\frac{1}{2}$in) deep. When the seedlings are 15cm (6in) high, they are ready to be transplanted to their permanent positions. Before doing so, firm the soil with your feet, give it a dressing of 112g per sq m (4oz per sq yd) of granular vegetable fertiliser, if this is considered

necessary, and rake it level. When transplanting, set the plants in holes 60cm (2ft) apart each way which have previously been filled with water, unless the soil is quite moist. The lowest pair of leaves on each plant should touch the soil, which should be firmed with your fingers. Hoe the soil regularly and water well in dry spells. Seedlings need protection from sparrows, while the mature crop is a favourite with wood pigeons. In windy areas draw soil up towards the stems or tie the stems to bamboo canes in the autumn.

Pests and diseases

Aphids, birds, caterpillars, club root, flea beetles and root fly.

Harvesting

Start to pick the sprouts at the bottom of the stem when they are golf-ball sized and still tightly closed. The sprouts should be pressed down and snapped off. This will encourage the sprouts further up the stem to mature. Store by freezing.

Cauliflower

Cauliflowers are such fine vegetables that growing them well gives the gardener immense satisfaction. Summer cauliflowers are in season from July to September; autumn varieties from October to December and winter cauliflowers from January to May.

Sowing and planting
All varieties require a soil which has been prepared in autumn or winter by digging in plenty of compost and liming it if necessary. Just before transplanting give the soil a dressing of 112g per sq m (4oz per sq yd) of granular vegetable fertiliser, unless the soil is well-enriched with organic matter. Summer varieties may be sown indoors in February and set outside in April to provide a July crop. Alternatively sow under cloches in March or in the open garden during the first half of April for cabbages in August. Autumn cauliflowers should be sown outdoors in April and May and transplanted in late June. Winter and spring varieties should be sown outdoors in May and transplanted in July. The seed outdoors should be sown 1cm ($\frac{1}{2}$in) deep. The seedlings are ready to transplant when they have six leaves. Set the plants in holes, which have been previously filled with water, if the soil is not naturally moist, 60cm (2ft) apart, at the same level as they were in the seed bed. It is vital to keep cauliflowers well watered especially in the early stages. If they wilt, they are unlikely later to produce firm tight heads. A light dressing of 28g (1oz) of nitrate of soda or nitro chalk may be given to each plant twice during its growing season as this improves the quality and quantity of the curds. Summer varieties should have a few leaves bent over the curds to protect them from the sun. With winter varieties, the same measure protects the curds from frost and snow.

Pests and diseases
Aphids, caterpillars, club root, flea beetle and root fly.

Harvesting
Cut cauliflowers while they are still small and tender. Summer and autumn varieties are at their best if cut in the morning with dew still on the curds. In frosty weather winter cauliflowers are best cut at midday. Cauliflowers hung upside down in a garage or shed remain in good condition for two weeks. Otherwise, store by freezing.

The cauliflower is a variety of cabbage which is cultivated for its undeveloped flower rather than its leaves. The flowers consist of extremely large white curds on thick succulent stems. They should be protected from strong sun and frost and snow alike, by bending a few leaves over the heads.

Cauliflower
Brassica oleracea Botrytis
(fam. *Cruciferae*)
Biennial
Size 45cm (18in) wide by 38cm (15in) high.
Edible part The curds.
Climate preferred Cool temperate to sub-tropical.
Aspect Open, but sheltered from cold northerly winds.
Sowing to harvest time 18 to 24 weeks for summer and autumn varieties; 40 weeks for winter and early spring varieties.
Yield 1kg (2lb) per plant.
Soil Rich loam, but sandy soils are suitable if plenty of organic material is dug in during winter.

Broccoli

Sowing and planting

Broccoli, to be successful, requires soil which has been well prepared with the addition of plenty of compost. The soil must also be firmed well with your feet before planting. Lime should be added in winter if necessary. The seed should be sown thinly in rows 1cm (½in) deep. Calabrese (green sprouting broccoli): sow in April or May and thin as soon as possible to prevent the plants from becoming weak through being over-crowded. When the seedlings are 8cm (3in) high, move them to their permanent positions with 45cm (18in) between the plants and 60cm (24in) between the rows. Before setting the plants in their final positions give the plot a dressing of 112g per sq m (4oz per sq yd) of granular vegetable fertiliser, if the soil is not already reasonably fertile. When transplanting, fill the planting holes with water if the soil is on the dry side. Allow the water to drain away. Then set the plants 2.5cm (1in) deeper in the holes than they were in the seed bed. Finally firm the soil around the plants with your fingers. Purple sprouting broccoli is the hardiest of the sprouting broccoli family and it does well in cold areas and on heavy clay soils where little else will grow over the winter. Sow the seeds, as before, in May and transplant when the seedlings are 8cm (3in) high to produce a crop from December to May, depending on the variety. White sprouting broccoli, sown at the same time, will produce its crop from March to May, depending on the variety. All broccoli requires regular hoeing to keep down weeds and plenty of water in long spells of dry weather in summer. Feed with nitro chalk, four weeks after transplanting, in rings around each plant at the rate of 28g per sq m (1oz per sq yd). With purple and white sprouting broccoli, draw soil up around the lower part of the stems in autumn to prevent their being felled by winter winds. Alternatively provide each plant with a bamboo stake.

Pests and diseases

Birds (especially wood pigeons), aphids, caterpillars, club root and root fly.

Harvesting

The time to cut broccoli is when the 'spears' are small and not too far developed; a point just before the small flower buds have opened. Cut the main centre spear first and then all the side spears, this will encourage lateral growth. Keep cutting and never let the plant flower or production of fresh spears will stop. Store by freezing.

Broccoli, Calabrese (green), purple and white sprouting

Brassica oleracea Botrytis (fam. *Cruciferae*)
Size 75cm (30in) high.
Edible part Flower buds with young leaves and stems; calabrese also forms an edible head.
Climate preferred Cool temperate to sub-tropical.
Aspect Open, but sheltered from winds.
Sowing to harvest time 12 weeks for calabrese; 40 weeks for purple and white varieties.
Yield 1kg (2lb) per plant.
Soil Heavy, firm and rich in organic matter.

Broccoli fresh from the garden is a real delight. Some people would say that it is a delicacy which rivals asparagus. Although closely related to the cauliflower, it is much easier to grow and can withstand greater extremes of heat and cold than cauliflowers or cabbages.

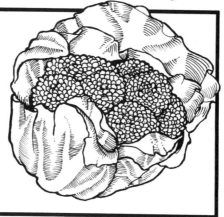

Spinach

Spinach is the sort of vegetable you either love or loathe. If you come into the first category, then growing lots of vitamin A and iron rich spinach is worthwhile, although it is not as easy to cultivate as some other vegetables. The trouble is that spinach has a tendency to run to seed at the expense of producing leaves. However, there are certain tricks to ensure constant success.

Sowing and planting

The soil for spinach must be deeply dug in winter and contain plenty of organic matter. Lime should also be added if necessary. Just before sowing time, as spinach is very greedy for plant foods, the soil may be given a dressing of granular vegetable fertiliser at the rate of 112g per sq m (4oz per sq yd). Ideally the plot for summer spinach should be in the light shade of other taller vegetables. Spinach can be intercropped between rows of peas and beans. Summer spinach should be sown every few weeks from March to mid July in rows 2.5cm (1in) deep and 30cm (12in) apart. Thin the seedlings as soon as they are large enough to handle to 8cm (3in) apart. Some weeks later, thin again to 15cm (6in) apart and retain the surplus plants for kitchen use. The remaining plants should be allowed to mature for use as required. Winter spinach should be sown in August—or September (in warm areas)—for picking between October and April. In cold districts it will be necessary to cover the crop with cloches in late autumn to protect it from frost. The soil around the plants must be hoed regularly to keep down weeds and to prevent its forming a crust. Constant supplies of water are essential during dry spells.

Pests and diseases

Aphids, damping off.

Harvesting

Cut away the outer leaves of plants with scissors as soon as they have reached an acceptable size. Continual picking will encourage fresh growth. With summer varieties, up to half the leaves can be removed at a picking. With winter varieties, remove only a quarter of the leaves at any one time. Store by freezing.

This page, above Spinach is a valuable source of vitamin A.

This page, below Ideally the plot for summer spinach should be in the light shade of other vegetables, such as between rows of beans.

Opposite page, top Sprouting broccoli does not produce solid heads but abundant spears.

Opposite page, bottom Calabrese is an Italian green broccoli which produces first a main head and then, when this is cut, smaller heads which sprout from the side.

Spinach

Spinacia oleracea (fam. *Chenopodiaceae*)
Annual
Size 30cm (1ft) high.
Edible part The leaves.
Climate preferred Cool temperate to sub-tropical depending on the variety.
Aspect Shaded for summer varieties; open but sheltered for winter varieties.
Sowing to harvest time 8 to 15 weeks.
Yield 225g (8oz) per plant.
Soil Deep, moist and rich in organic matter.

Spinach, New Zealand

Right *New Zealand spinach will thrive in climates too hot or too dry for ordinary spinach.*

Below *Spinach beet will tolerate extremes of climate and poor soils.*

Spinach, New Zealand

Tetragonia expansa (fam. *Aizoaceae*)
Annual
Size 60cm (2ft) wide and spreading.
Edible part Leaves.
Climate preferred Cool temperate to sub-tropical.
Aspect Sheltered.
Yield 1kg (2lb) per plant, but the more you pick the more the plant will produce.
Planting to harvest time 8 to 10 weeks.
Soil Deep, moist and rich in organic matter.

New Zealand 'spinach' is not strictly a spinach at all. Nevertheless, it is a very good substitute in parts of the world where it is too hot for ordinary spinach or the summers are too dry for successful spinach growing. Though tolerant of droughts, the leaves will be more succulent if you water regularly.

Sowing and planting
The soil should be prepared as for ordinary spinach. In mid May the seeds should be soaked in water overnight to soften them and so speed germination. Then they should be sown in clusters of three in rows 1cm ($\frac{1}{2}$in) deep with 60cm (2ft) between subsequent clusters and other rows. As soon as the seedlings are large enough to handle, thin to leave just one plant 60cm (2ft) apart. Hoe to keep down weeds and water well. When the plants measure 30cm (1ft) across, remove the growing points to encourage the formation of more young leaves.

Pests and diseases
None of any consequence.

Harvesting
Cut a few leaves regularly from each plant near to the base of the stalks to encourage the plant to continue producing fresh young leaves. Start picking as soon as the leaves are of usable size.

Spinach, beet

Spinach beet (also called perpetual spinach)

Beta vulgaris (fam. *Chenopodiaceae*)
Hardy perennial with a useful life of one year
Size 30cm (12in) high.
Edible part The leaves.
Climate preferred Cool temperate to sub-tropical.
Aspect Open or slightly shaded.
Planting to harvest time 8 to 14 weeks.
Yield $\frac{1}{2}$kg (1lb) per plant but the more you pick the more you get.
Soil Deep, moist and rich in organic matter, but unlike ordinary spinach will tolerate poor or sandy soil.

Spinach beet has the advantages that it does not bolt in summer or die of cold in winter. Its mild taste is also found more acceptable by children.

Sowing and planting
The soil should be prepared as for ordinary spinach. In April sow the seeds in 2.5cm (1in) deep drills, 45cm (18in) apart. Thin the seedlings as soon as they are large enough to handle to 20cm (8in) apart.

Pests and diseases
Virtually trouble free.

Harvesting
The first leaves can be removed from the outside of the plants in summer, but go easy. The real point of spinach beet is to enable you to have spinach in winter and spring when the ordinary kind is scarce. Although the beets would con-tinue cropping for a couple of years or so, it is more satisfactory to raise a fresh crop annually.

Seakale beet

Seakale beet is easily grown and it provides a continuous supply of spinach-like greens throughout the summer and autumn, even during droughts. Although it is a form of beet, there is no edible root. Instead it produces large, glossy leaves with thick mid-ribs. The leaves are cooked like ordinary spinach and the mid-ribs like asparagus. Alternatively both can be cooked together.

Sowing and planting

The soil should be prepared as for ordinary spinach. In April sow three seeds together 1cm ($\frac{1}{2}$in) deep every 38cm (15in) in drills 45cm (18in) apart. As soon as the seedlings can be handled easily, thin to leave the strongest one every 38cm (15in) apart. The aftercare of seakale beet is the same as for spinach.

Pests and diseases

Virtually trouble free.

Harvesting

It is essential to remove the stems from the outside of each plant to enable the central stems to develop. The stems should be pulled like rhubarb as cutting makes them bleed. If the beets can be covered with cloches over the winter, there will be a fresh crop of leaves for the following spring, summer and autumn. Otherwise sow again in April.

Above *Seakale beet is a dual purpose vegetable in that the mid-ribs may be removed and cooked separately.*

Below *Pick the outside leaves first and never cut them.*

Seakale Beet

Beta vulgaris Cicla (fam. *Chenopodiaceae*)
Perennial with a useful life of normally one year
Size 45cm (18in) high and 30cm (12in) wide.
Edible parts The stems and leaves.
Climate preferred Cool temperate to sub-tropical.
Aspect Sun or sahde.
Planting to harvest time 12 weeks.
Yield 1$\frac{1}{2}$kg (3lb) a plant but the more you harvest the more you get.
Soil Moist with added organic matter, but will also grow in light sandy soil and heavy clay.

Pea, asparagus

Above *Asparagus peas are easy to grow and a pleasure to eat.*

Opposite page *The garden pea is highly nutritious.*

Pea, asparagus

Tetragonolobus purpureus
(fam. *Leguminosae*)
Half-hardy annual
Size 30cm (12in) high.
Edible part The seed pods.
Climate preferred Temperate to sub-tropical.
Aspect Sunny and sheltered.
Sowing to harvest time 14 to 16 weeks.
Yield 1½kg to 2kg (3 to 4½lb) to a 3m (10ft) row.
Soil Well drained and rich in humus.

Asparagus peas belong to the same family as garden peas, but there any similarity ends. The pods of these particular peas have wavy flanges like wings. Hence the asparagus pea's other name, the winged pea. The flavour has a delicate hint of asparagus, and, in common with the mangetout, the pods are cooked whole. The plants bear delightful sweet-pea like scarlet flowers and are sufficiently attractive to be grown anywhere in the garden.

Sowing and planting

The soil for asparagus peas should be prepared in exactly the same way as for garden peas. The seeds should be sown 1cm (½in) deep and 10cm (4in) apart in rows 45cm (18in) apart in late April in mild districts and elsewhere in May. Cover with cloches at first, if you have

them. Thin to 20cm (8in) apart when the plants can be handled easily. In exposed areas the plants may need supporting with twiggy brushwood or staking with bamboo canes. The aftercare of asparagus peas is exactly the same as for garden peas remembering to hoe regularly and water in dry weather.

Pests and diseases

Aphids, birds and pea moth although these occur very rarely.

Harvesting

Start to pick the pods when they are about 4cm (1½in) long. Do not wait until the pods have reached their full length of 8cm (3in) or you will lose a lot of the flavour. By gathering continually it is possible to harvest for a couple of months. Store by freezing.

Pea,garden

Peas are popular, but are tricky to grow. However the thrill of eating sweet green peas fresh from the garden makes all the effort worthwhile. Of the ordinary garden type, there are round varieties which are very hardy and the quickest of peas to mature. Then there are the wrinkle-seeded peas, which are sweeter and heavier cropping than the round varieties. The French varieties of wrinkle-seeded pea are known as petit pois. Finally there are the sugar pea varieties, also called mangetout or snow peas. These are harvested before the pea is fully formed and the whole shell is eaten.

Sowing and planting

Ideally the site chosen for peas should not have grown this crop for two consecutive years. The soil should be dug over in autumn or winter and plenty of compost should be worked in. If necessary, lime can be added as peas prefer an alkaline soil. About a week before sowing the soil may be given a dressing of granular fertiliser at the rate of 56g per sq m (2oz per sq yd). Then rake the soil back and forth to provide a good tilth. The varieties of peas that you sow will largely be determined by the time you wish the crop to mature. For instance, for peas in May and June, you should sow a round variety in either October or November and cover with cloches. For peas in June and July, you should sow a round or an early variety of wrinkle-seeded pea in March or April. For peas in August, sow a maincrop wrinkled variety in April or May. This is also the time to sow French petit pois and sugar peas. For peas in September, sow a wrinkled variety in June or July. The technique of sowing peas is the same for all varieties. Make a drill 15cm (6in) wide and 5cm (2in) deep. The seeds are then placed by hand in three staggered rows in this drill so that each seed is approximately 8cm (3in) apart from its neighbours. Subsequent drills of peas should be a distance apart equal to the eventual height of the crop. So if you were growing Green Shaft, for example, which is 75cm (2½ft) tall, your second drill would be 75cm (2½ft) away from the first. Newly sown seeds, unless covered with cloches, should be protected with plastic netting or wire netting guards. Hoe the soil regularly to prevent it caking, and to keep weeds under control. When the pea plants are 15cm (6in) high, insert twiggy branches along the outer sides of the drills to provide support. Dwarf varieties will not require any

further assistance, but medium and tall varieties, especially those of the sugar pea, will require plastic netting erected close to the drill for support. In June, put down a 5cm (2in) moisture-retaining and weed-suppressing mulch of peat around the drills of peas. Watering during dry spells is vital to swell the pods.

Pests and diseases

Aphids, birds and pea moth. Seedlings should be protected from slugs.

Harvesting

Pick the pods from the bottom of the plants when they appear well filled. The mangetout, or sugar peas, should be picked when the pods are fleshy, but before the shape of the peas can be seen in the pods. Store your surplus crop of peas or mangetout by freezing.

Pea, garden (including petit pois) and sugar peas

Pisum sativum and *P. sativum* Saccharatum (fam. *Leguminosæ*)
Hardy annual
Size Dwarf varieties are 45cm (18in). Others are up to 150cm (5ft) high.
Edible part The peas, garden variety; the pods, sugar variety.
Climate preferred Cool temperate.
Aspect Open.
Planting to harvest time 32 weeks for autumn sowings; 14 to 16 weeks for spring sowings.
Yield 2kg to 4½kg (4 to 10lb) to a 3m (10ft) row, depending on the variety.
Soil Well drained and rich in humus.

Bean, broad

These are the best choice for hardiness, top yields and early crops. The Windsor varieties, which are distinguished by their shorter, wider pods. These are the best choice for flavour and later crops, but they cannot be sown in autumn. The Dwarf varieties, which have short pods and dwarf bushy growth, ideal for small gardens where the space for vegetables is limited. They are normally grown in single rows.

Sowing and planting
The soil should be well dug and compost should be added if necessary. About a week before sowing a dressing of granular fertiliser may be applied at the rate of 112g per sq m (4oz per sq yd). In mild areas, the long pod varieties can be sown in November 5cm (2in) deep with 15cm (6in) between the seeds. A second row should be sown just 23cm (9in) away. Subsequent sets of 'double rows' should be 60cm (2ft) away. If possible cover with cloches during winter. All varieties can also be sown in March and April. Water and weed regularly.

Pests and diseases
Aphids (particularly blackfly), botrytis (grey mould), and slugs.

Harvesting
Pick the pods while the scar on each bean in the shell is green or white (*not* black) for top flavour. Store by freezing.

Bean, broad
Vicia faba (fam. *Leguminosae*)
Annual
Size 1.2m by 25cm (4ft by 10in). Dwarf varieties are 30cm to 40cm by 25cm (12in to 18in by 10in).
Edible part The beans, but pods and beans can be eaten if picked while small.
Climate preferred Cool temperate.
Aspect Open.
Planting to harvest time 16 weeks for spring sowings; 28 weeks for autumn sowings.
Yield 5kg (11lb) to a 3m (10ft) double row. Dwarf varieties, 2kg (4½lb) to a single row.
Soil Ordinary, but well drained.

Broad beans are one of the easiest vegetables to grow and are very tasty if picked fresh. There are three main types. The Longpod varieties, which can be recognised by their long, narrow pods.

Bean, butter or lima

Butter or lima beans are widely grown in the United States and Canada, but they are a comparatively new crop to Britain. The latest varieties produce fine crops of delicious green lima beans, and in most summers the ripened butter beans as well. Such beans, fresh from the garden, have a taste almost like that of chestnuts. The dried beans, however, are handy for winter soups and stews.

Sowing and planting
The seeds should be sown singly in 8cm (3in) wide peat pots containing peat-based compost in mid May. Place them in a warm dark spot indoors to germinate. The minimum temperature required is 21°C (70°F). The plants should be ready to set outdoors from mid to late June. The soil for lima or butter beans should be prepared by digging in plenty of compost and dressing with a granular vegetable fertiliser at the rate of 112g per sq m (4oz per sq yd). Dwarf varieties should be set out 15cm (6in) apart in rows 60cm (2ft) apart. Climbing varieties should be 15cm (6in) apart in rows 1.2m (4ft) apart. Bush varieties can manage with just a few twiggy sticks for support, but climbing types need stout posts and plastic bean netting. Keep the soil well hoed to prevent it forming a crust and provide plenty of water in dry spells. Do not be tempted to give any extra feeding to the beans as too much nitrogen fertiliser results in leafy growth at the expense of pods.

Pests and diseases
Aphid, capsid, botrytis and slugs.

Harvesting
Beans picked when they are young and tender can be used in the same way as French beans. Otherwise the beans should be allowed to ripen until about two weeks before you expect the first frost. Mature beans should be shelled, dried and stored in ventilated cardboard boxes, or frozen.

Bean, butter or lima
Phaseolus lunatus limensis (fam. *Leguminosae*)
Annual
Size Bush varieties 45cm (18in) high. Climbing varieties 1.8m (6ft) high.
Edible part Tender young beans can be eaten like French beans. Mature beans are eaten without their pods.
Climate preferred Temperate to sub-tropical.
Aspect Sunny and sheltered.
Planting to harvest time 16 to 22 weeks.
Yield 2kg (4lb) to a 3m (10ft) row.
Soil Medium to light and well drained.

Bean, French and haricot

The French and the haricot bean are different forms of one plant. The young, whole bean, including the pod is called a French bean. The ripe seeds of the discarded pod are haricot beans.

Sowing and planting
The soil should be thoroughly dug over and organic matter and lime added as necessary. About a week before sowing the soil may be given a dressing of 112g per sq m (4oz per sq yd) of granular fertiliser, which should be worked in lightly with a hoe. Then the soil should be raked to produce a fine tilth. If you have cloches, you can begin by sowing the seeds in April in rows 5cm (2in) deep and 60cm (2ft) apart. The seeds should be spaced 8cm (3in) apart in the rows and later thinned to 15cm (6in) apart. Without cloches you can make successional sowings from May to early June. If cloches are available, a sowing can be made in July to provide a late autumn crop. The cloches will be required to cover the beans in October. The plants may need support from short twiggy branches or sticks. Climbing varieties will need the support of plastic bean netting or sticks. Hoe and water regularly.

At the end of the season allow the remaining seeds to ripen in order to produce haricot beans. These can be used either as seeds for a new crop or for cooking.

Pests and diseases
Aphids, capsid, botrytis and slugs (particular problem with seedlings).

Harvesting
The pods are ready for picking from about 10cm (4in) long when they snap easily if bent. Do not wait until the bulges of beans are visible in the pods. Harvest several times a week if necessary so that the plants will continue to crop for six to eight weeks. Store by freezing.

To harvest haricot beans, however, the remaining beans must be left to ripen. In late summer or early autumn when the plants are light brown in colour, dry and brittle, pull the entire plants out of the ground and hang them up indoors, or in a sunny position in the garden, to dry. After about a week, when the pods become brittle, shell the beans and leave them to dry spread out on newspaper for a few days. The dried beans are best stored in ventilated cardboard boxes.

Above *The haricot bean is the ripe seed of the French bean. It is high in protein and vitamins and low in calories, which makes it ideal for those on a diet.*

Opposite page *The broad bean is the hardiest member of the bean family. Like all pulses it nourishes the soil by replacing nitrogen.*

Bean, French and haricot

Phaseolus vulgaris (fam. *Leguminosae*)
Annual
Size 30cm (12in) high, dwarf varieties; 1.5m (5ft) high, climbing varieties.
Edible part The pods.
Climate preferred Cool temperate to sub-tropical.
Aspect Open and sunny.
Planting to harvest time 10 to 14 weeks.
Yield 3kg (6½lb) to 3m (10ft) row, dwarf varieties; 4½kg (10lb) to a 3m (10ft) row, climbing varieties.
Soil Light and well drained.

Bean, runner

A native of tropical America, the runner bean nevertheless thrives in cooler climates as well.

Bean, runner

Phaseolus coccineus (fam. *Leguminosae*)

Perennial grown as an annual

Size Climbing varieties are 2.4m to 3m (8 to 10ft) high; dwarf varieties are 45cm (18in) high.

Edible part The pods.

Climate preferred Cool temperate to sub-tropical.

Aspect Open, sunny and sheltered from winds.

Planting to harvest time 12 to 16 weeks.

Yield 18kg (40lb) to a 3m (10ft) row, climbing varieties; 8kg (17½lb) to a 3m (10ft) row, dwarf varieties.

Soil Moist, containing plenty of humus. Heavy clay and sandy soils are unsuitable.

Runner beans are possibly the most prolific crop in the vegetable garden. They are also one of the most attractive with their scarlet flowers among the lush green leaves. The most common varieties are the stick or pole runner beans, which can produce pods up to 50cm (20in) long. However, there are also dwarf runner beans with pods just 20cm (8in) long which are most suitable in small gardens or in cold, windy situations.

Sowing and planting

The position for runner beans should be prepared in winter by digging over an area 45cm (18in) wide and the depth of the spade and incorporating a thick layer of compost in the bottom. In mild areas the seeds can be sown outdoors at the end of May 5cm (2in) deep and 23cm (9in) apart with 38cm (15in) between the first and second row. At each 23cm (9in) interval two seeds should be placed to allow for losses and the weaker seedlings remaining should be removed soon after germination. Subsequent double rows of beans should be 1.5m (5ft) away. In cold districts it is better to sow the seeds indoors or in a cold frame or greenhouse in early May. Sow the seeds individually in peat pots containing peat-based compost and do not plant outdoors until the roots are growing strongly through the sides of the pots. Climbing beans will require support from poles or stout bamboo canes inserted into the soil so that they form an inverted 'V' shape. Alternatively use netting supported by strong posts. Dwarf beans may also need support, from short twigs. Tie the plants, loosely at first, to their supports. Once they start to grow, they will climb by themselves. Hoe the soil regularly and keep the plants clear of weeds. Copious watering is required in dry spells, and the flowers, when they appear, should be sprayed gently with water in the evenings to encourage pods to form. A moisture-retaining and weed-suppressing mulch of peat can be put down around the plants in July. In late July, and again in August, feed the plants with liquid fertiliser. Once the plants have reached the tops of their supports remove their growing points.

Pests and diseases

Seeds may be eaten by slugs and millepedes. Mature plants may be attacked by aphids, and capsids and botrytis in wet summers.

Harvesting

Pick the pods when they are young and tender and do not wait until they are long and 'stringy' with the seeds bulging in the pods. By regular picking of small beans you should be able to harvest fresh for more than six weeks. Store the surplus crop by freezing or by salting.

Sweetcorn

Sweetcorn is as American as blueberry pie and it is something which for years had to be imported to Europe. If you have only had sweetcorn from a supermarket, then you are in for a real treat when you harvest those first cobs from the garden. Fresh sweetcorn is as different from the shop-bought kind as champagne is from sparkling wine.

Sowing and planting
The soil should be well dug and enriched with organic matter. Just before planting 112g per sq m (4oz per sq yd) of granular vegetable fertiliser may be lightly forked or raked into the soil. Ideally the sweetcorn plants should be raised by sowing the seeds individually, 2.5cm (1in) deep in 8cm (3in) wide peat pots containing peat-based compost, between mid April and early May. The pots must be kept in either a greenhouse or indoors on a kitchen window sill until the risk of frost has passed, in late May or early June. Alternatively, if you live in a mild district, you can sow the seeds directly outdoors in mid May. Two seeds should be sown together 2.5cm (1in) deep every 45cm (18in), along rows spaced 45cm (18in) apart. Since sweetcorn is pollinated by the wind, it is essential that you have at least four rows, no matter how short, so that you have a block of plants, providing the maximum amount of pollen. Once the outdoor seedlings are large enough to handle, thin to leave the strongest plants 45cm (18in) apart. The plants in peat pots should be set out 45cm (18in) apart each way in holes which have previously been filled with water. Since the roots of sweetcorn are very close to the surface, a moisture-retaining and weed-suppressing mulch of peat is beneficial. In any case, do not hoe between the plants; it is better to let the weeds grow than to destroy the roots of the sweetcorn. Water copiously in dry spells.

Pests and diseases
None of any consequence.

Harvesting
Your first indication that the cobs are ripening is when the silks at the tops of the green-sheathed cobs turn brown. The next step is to make the thumb-nail test. Pull back part of the sheath and squeeze a couple of corn grains between finger and thumbnail. If the liquid exuded is watery, the cob is not yet ripe. If the liquid is creamy, then you have cobs perfect for picking. If the liquid is doughy, then they are overripe and the cobs are not fit for eating. The ripe cobs should be twisted free from the plant. Store the surplus crop by freezing.

Although strictly a cereal, sweetcorn is regarded as a vegetable. It is very important to establish the correct stage of maturity before harvesting.

Sweetcorn

Zea mays saccharata (fam. *Gramineae*)
Annual
Size 1m to 1.8m (3ft to 6ft) tall.
Edible part The seed cobs.
Climate preferred Temperate to sub-tropical.
Aspect Sheltered and sunny.
Sowing to harvest time 12 to 16 weeks.
Yield Usually one cob per plant.
Soil type Any soil provided it is enriched with organic matter.

Potato

Above *There are numerous varieties of potatoes, all subtly different in flavour and texture to suit your requirements.*

Right *To dig up the roots, plunge a fork deeply into the soil about 25cm (10in) from the plant and force it upwards. Grasp the crown to pull away the tubers.*

Potato

Solanum tuberosum (fam. *Solanaceae*)

Half-hardy perennial, but treated as an annual

Size The haulms may be 60cm to 90cm (2ft to 3ft) high.

Edible part The tubers.

Climate preferred Cool temperate to sub-tropical.

Aspect Open.

Planting to harvest time Early varieties, 14 weeks; maincrop varieties 20 to 22 weeks.

Yield 6kg to 10kg (13lb to 22lb) to a 3m (10ft) row.

Soil Most soils are suitable.

The potato is a superb vegetable which is universally popular. There are varieties which yield potatoes that are white and floury and ideal for mashing or baking. There are others which produce waxy potatoes ideal for salads. New potatoes, fresh from the soil, are especially rich in vitamin C and they have a flavour few shop-bought potatoes can equal.

Sowing and Planting

Potatoes are the crop to grow if you want to turn grassland or wasteland into a vegetable plot or garden as explained in the first chapter. But having said that, even the roughest and most neglected of soils will be all the better with the standard soil treatment for potatoes. If possible, choose a sunny spot for potato growing and dig the soil in the autumn, incorporating as much compost, or peat, as you can spare. However, on no account add lime as lime causes crops to be small. Ideally, you should obtain your seed potatoes in February and place them rose end (that is the bit with most of the shoots or 'eyes') uppermost in seed trays, or empty egg cartons, which

should be placed in a cool, airy, light, but not sunny, spot such as a shed or garage so that the potatoes can start to sprout. A 9m (30ft) row, or three 3m (10ft) rows, will require 2¼kg (5lb) of seed potatoes. The time to plant the seed potatoes outdoors will be determined by how late you can expect your last frost. But, generally, early varieties are planted between mid March and mid April. Maincrop varieties are planted at the same time. To plant potatoes make V-shaped drills about 13cm (5in) deep and 60cm (24in) apart for early varieties, 45cm (30in) apart for maincrop varieties. The early varieties need be no more than 30cm (12in) apart in the drills; maincrop varieties should be 38cm (15in) apart. The seed potatoes should be set in the drills, rose end uppermost, and first covered with a little peat, compost or fine soil to prevent damage to the new shoots. The drills should then be filled in so that a slight ridge is left along them. After planting, granular vegetable fertiliser may be scattered over the drills at the rate of 112g per sq m (4oz per sq yd). If there is still a risk of frost when the first shoots appear from the soil, draw a little earth over them for protection. When the shoots reach 23cm (9in) high, the process called 'earthing-up' begins. Fork the soil lightly between the rows, and using your spade, pile the loose soil against the stems to produce a ridge 15cm (6in) high. Keep the weeds down between the rows with your hoe and flood with water in dry weather.

Pests and diseases

Aphids, scab, (grow resistant varieties) wart disease (grow immune varieties), wireworm and blight. The last disease named is peculiar to potatoes. The disease can be distinguished by brown markings on the leaves and by the fact that the haulm also collapses. The tubers develop sunken areas which are reddish brown beneath the surface. The preventative treatment for affected areas (as not all districts suffer from blight) is to spray with Bordeaux powder from early July at least three times at two week intervals. As blight largely affects maincrop potatoes, the solution in areas susceptible to the disease is to grow only early varieties which can be lifted before the July danger period.

Harvesting

Early varieties can be lifted when the flowers wither. Insert your fork into the soil well away from the haulm and then lift the haulm and its roots away from the row. Give the haulm a shake and most of the potatoes will fall away cleanly. When the haulms of maincrop varieties have withered in September or October, cut off the stems and remove them. Then wait for 10 days and lift the entire crop. The potatoes should be allowed to dry before storing them in hessian sacks, or in slatted wooden boxes in a dark, frost-free place.

Artichoke, Jerusalem

The Jerusalem artichoke has a most puzzling name. One might assume that it originated in the Middle East. Yet is has nothing to do with that Jerusalem. The plant, a relative of the sunflower, is a native of North America and how it came to be named is still one of gardening's unsolved mysteries. It is very easy to grow, either in the vegetable garden or herbaceous border, and it makes a very useful screen. The white-skinned varieties have a slightly better flavour than those with purple skins.

Planting

The soil for Jerusalem artichokes should be prepared by digging in either compost or peat to lighten it. No fertilisers are required as these would encourage the formation of leaves at the expense of tubers. It is essential to plant well away from other crops because of the shade cast by the tall foliage. Plant the tubers at the end of February or early in March 8cm (3in) deep and 38cm (15in) apart with 90cm (3ft) between the rows. The soil should be kept well hoed and weed free. Water should be given in dry spells. Occasionally use the hoe to draw soil up towards the stems to make ridges. In windy situations, support the plants by stretching wires between 1.8m (6ft) posts. At the end of October, cut all the top growth down to ground level.

Pests and diseases

Slugs may feed on tubers and young shoots, if not protected.

Harvesting

The tubers can be lifted as required in autumn or winter, or lift the entire crop in autumn and store in the same way as potatoes. If even one tuber is left in the soil, it will shoot up the next year. Once the tubers have been exposed to light, they should be cooked as soon as possible to prevent discolouration.

Propagation

A few tubers should be retained for planting in the spring, elsewhere in the garden. The reason for planting the tubers in a new site is that, although they will grow successfully in the same place, if left the roots tend to spread and become very entangled.

Artichoke, Jerusalem

Helianthus tuberosus (fam. *Compositae*)
Hardy perennial with a useful life of one year
Size 2m to 3.6m (7ft to 12ft) tall by 60cm (2ft) wide.
Edible part The tubers.
Climate preferred Cool temperate to sub-tropical.
Aspect Open or partially shaded.
Planting to harvest time 8 to 10 months.
Yield 1kg to 2kg (2lb to 4½lb) of edible tubers per plant.
Soil Ordinary, provided it is well drained.

Onion family

Onion

Onion, bulb varieties, salad and pickling

Allium cepa (fam. *Alliaceae*)
Biennial
Size 25cm to 45cm (10in to 18in) tall with 8cm to 15cm (3in to 6in) spread.
Edible part The bulbs and stems.
Climate preferred Cool temperate to sub-tropical.
Aspect Open and sunny.
Planting/sowing to harvest time Onions raised from seed take 44 weeks if August sown, 22 weeks if spring sown; onions raised from sets take 18 weeks. Spring onions take 10 to 12 weeks. Pickling onions take 22 weeks.
Yield 3½kg (8lb) of bulbs from seed or sets to a 3m (10ft) row; 2kg (4½lb) pickling onions to a 3m (10ft) row and 1kg (2lb) spring onions to a 3m (10ft) row.
Soil Well drained, light and rich in organic matter.

Onions are a most useful crop as they store so easily. The bulbs have so many culinary uses from salads to stews and soups to sauces. You can fry them, pickle them, boil and roast them. What more could one ask of a vegetable?

Sowing and planting

The soil should be prepared by digging in plenty of compost and dressing, where necessary, with vegetable fertiliser at the rate of 112g per sq m (4oz per sq yd). When the soil is dry, tread it firm and then rake it carefully to produce a good tilth. In mild districts, the seed can be sown in August to produce tiny bulbs for transplanting in March and a crop in July. Elsewhere the seed can be sown in March or April to produce a late August or September crop. The seed should be sown very thinly 1cm (½in) deep in rows 30cm (12in) apart. Seedlings from an August sowing should be transplanted to 15cm (6in) apart with 30cm (12in) between the rows. Spring sown onions should be thinned first to 5cm (2in) and

later to 15cm (6in) apart, retaining 30cm (12in) between the rows. The thinnings can be used as 'spring onions' for salads. However it is better to use a special variety for this purpose. The seeds should be sown as for ordinary onions, except that the rows need be just 15cm (6in) apart and the seedlings are not thinned. With spring onions successional sowings at approximately fortnightly intervals are essential to produce plenty of delicately flavoured young plants. Pickling onions are sown in the same way in rows 25cm (10in) apart and like spring onions are not thinned. To produce a crop of onions from the little bulbs, called sets, the soil should be prepared carefully as for seed sowing. Each bulb should be pushed into the soil so that its neck is barely visible. The bulbs should be 15cm (6in) apart with 30cm (12in) between the rows. All onions should be kept free from weeds and watered regularly. An additional feed of 56g per sq m (2oz per sq yd) of granular vegetable fertiliser can be given

in May and hoed in lightly to increase the size of the bulbs. Snap off any flower heads which may appear. Stop watering as the bulbs begin to ripen and draw the soil away from the bulbs to enable the sun to reach them.

Pests and diseases
Onion fly (but sets are generally free from attack). Birds may pull sets from the ground (the remedy is to snip off

loose skin from the neck of the bulbs before planting).

Harvesting
When the leaves have toppled over and started to yellow, the crop can be lifted and allowed to dry on a wire netting cradle a few inches from the ground. Store by plaiting with raffia or by hanging in plastic netting in a dry shed, cellar or garage.

Left *When the lower leaves begin to topple over and turn yellow the onion crop is ready for lifting.*

Shallot

Shallots have a milder flavour than onions and are very good for pickling. Unlike the onion, which grows bigger as it matures, the shallot produces new clumps of bulbs around the original set.

Shallot

Allium ascalonicum (fam. *Alliaceae*)
Biennial
Size Forms a clump 10cm to 15cm (4in to 6in) wide and 45cm (18in) high.
Edible part The bulbs.
Climate preferred Cool temperate to sub-tropical.
Aspect Open and sunny.
Planting to harvest time 10 to 25 weeks.
Yield 4½kg (10lb) to a 3m (10ft) row.
Soil Well drained and rich in organic matter.

Shallots are easy to grow and make a mild alternative to onions. They are also good for pickling. Unlike onions which produced a single bulb, shallots grow into clumps of little bulbs around the original 'set'.

Planting
In late autumn or early winter dig over the soil and fork in compost. Early in February the soil may be given a dressing of granular vegetable fertiliser at the rate of 56g per sq m (2oz per sq yd). Hoe this in and at the same time attempt to get the soil into a good tilth. In mid February or before mid March, push the bulbs into the soil so that their necks are barely visible. The bulbs should be 15cm to 20cm (6in to 8in) apart in rows 30cm (12in) apart. Hoe carefully to avoid damage to the bulbs and water only when absolutely necessary. In June scrape some soil away from the bulb clusters to expose them to the sun and so assist ripening. Immature shallots which are exposed should be replanted.

Pests and diseases
Shallots suffer from the same problems as onions.

Harvesting
As soon as the foliage has yellowed in June or July, dig up the shallots and dry them on a wire netting cradle a few inches from the ground. When dried, rub off any dead foliage and loose skin. Put aside some of the bulbs for next year's crop. The others can be stored in plastic netting in shed or garage. Remember to examine them from time to time and remove any of the shallots which look as if they are going bad.

Propagation
Medium-sized, healthy bulbs can be used to provide the following year's supply of shallots for planting.

Leek

The leek is a splendid choice of vegetable for gardeners living in areas where the growing conditions are poor. So little can go wrong that even someone new to gardening is bound to be successful.

Sowing and planting
Ideally the soil for leeks should have been enriched with compost for a previous crop such as early peas or potatoes. If not, work in some well-rotted compost, alternatively work in peat and apply a dressing of granular general fertiliser at the rate of 112g per sq m (4oz per sq yd) two weeks before planting. The seed should be sown outdoors in a nursery bed 1cm (½in) deep in rows 20cm (8in) apart between early March and mid April. The seedlings are ready for transplanting in June or July when they are 20cm (8in) high. They should be set out in rows 30cm (12in) apart with 15cm (6in) between the plants.

Transplanting calls for a special procedure: 15cm (6in) deep holes are made for the leeks with a dibber or stick; the plants are dropped in the holes; the holes are then filled with water which settles soil around the roots. There is no need to fill the holes with soil. The plants should be kept weed free by frequent hoeing and water should be given in summer whenever the weather is dry. Soil can be drawn up against the stems of the plants as they develop if you wish your leeks to be well blanched.

Pests and diseases
Virtually none.

Harvesting
Lift the leeks out of the soil with a fork when they are fully developed throughout winter and spring. Since leeks can remain in the soil throughout the winter months, harvest as required.

The leek has the most subtle flavour of the onion family. If you wish your leeks to be well blanched, you should draw the soil up against the stems to form a trench. Keep free from weeds.

Leek

Allium porrum (fam. *Alliaceae*)
Biennial grown as an annual
Size 30 to 38cm (12 to 15 in) tall.
Edible part The stems.
Climate preferred Cool temperate to sub-tropical.
Aspect Open.
Sowing to harvest time 35 weeks, early varieties; 45 weeks, late varieties.
Yield 5kg (11lb) to a 3m (10ft) row.
Soil Ordinary, provided it is well drained.

Root vegetables

Carrot

Carrots are one of the easiest of vegetables to grow. Forget what you may have heard about their requiring sandy soil. The trick is to suit the varieties of carrots to your soil. For instance, round and short-rooted kinds are the best choice for stony soil or clay. Stump-rooted kinds will suit the majority of soils and those long-rooted types are best left to the people with sandy soils or an eye on a prize at the local horticultural show.

Sowing and planting

Like all root crops, carrots do best in soil which has been well-prepared for a previous crop. Otherwise the soil should be prepared by deep digging in autumn or winter and dressed with granular vegetable fertiliser at the rate of 112g per sq m (4oz per sq yd) two weeks before sowing. Do not add any organic matter. Early varieties can be sown initially in March under cloches and at fortnightly intervals to mid April. Sowings of maincrop varieties can begin in mid April and continue at intervals until mid July. Before sowing, rake the soil carefully to produce a good tilth. The drills should be just 1cm (½in) deep and dusted lightly with Gamma-BHC as a precaution against carrot fly before sowing. The seed should be sown as thinly as possible to cut down on the need for thinning later. If you wish to avoid this chore, use pelleted seed and place the pellets at 2.5cm (1in) intervals. Cover the drills with sifted soil and firm the surface with the flat head of a rake. Subsequent drills of early varieties should be 20cm (8in) apart; maincrop should be 30cm (12in) apart. Thin out the seedlings as soon as they are large enough to handle to 5cm (2in) apart and later to 10cm (4in) apart. The second thinnings will provide some usable little carrots. Water in dry spells and use the hoe to keep down weeds.

Pests and diseases

Aphids (leaves turn red and plants are stunted) and carrot fly.

Harvesting

The crop can be lifted as required. Maincrop carrots can be lifted for storage in October. Choose a dry day and rub excess soil off lightly. Cut the foliage back to about 1cm (½in) above the crowns. Then store the carrots in layers in boxes with slightly moist peat between the layers.

Above *Planting carrots between rows of onions helps mask the aroma of the foliage which attracts the carrot fly.*

Opposite page *For perfect roots, never sow carrots in recently manured soil.*

Carrot

Daucus carota (fam. *Umbelliferae*)
Biennial grown as an annual
Size Roots can be round and about 4cm (1½in) in diameter, short or stump-rooted and about 10cm (4in) long, or long-rooted and tapering, measuring 15cm (6in) and more.
Edible part The root.
Climate preferred Cool temperate to sub-tropical.
Aspect Open and sunny, or partial shade.
Sowing to harvest time 15 weeks, early varieties; 18 weeks, maincrop.
Yield Early varieties, 2kg (4½lb) to a 3m (10ft) row; maincrop, 4kg (9lb) to a 3m (10ft) row.
Soil Deep light loam, but any soil can be made suitable.

Salsify

Left *Take great care when lifting salsify as damaged roots are liable to bleed.*

Right *An unusual vegetable with a delicate flavour.*

Salsify/Scorzonera

Tragopogon porrifolius and *Scorzonera hispanica* (fam. *Compositae*)
Biennial grown as an annual
Size About 30cm (1ft) long.
Edible part The root.
Climate preferred Temperate to sub-tropical.
Aspect Open and sunny, or partially shaded.
Sowing to harvest time 26 to 30 weeks.
Yield 3kg (6½lb) to a 3m (10ft) row.
Soil Any soil, provided it is rich in humus and well drained.

Salsify, which is white-skinned, has a distinctive, somewhat fishy taste. Hence its other name: the vegetable oyster. Scorzonera, which has black skin, has a similar flavour and both vegetables make delicious additions to winter meals.

Sowing and planting

The soil for both salsify and scorzonera should be prepared by deep digging. If possible, remove any large stones which could cause the roots to fork. Two weeks before sowing (early April for salsify, late April for scorzonera) the soil may be dressed if necessary with granular general fertiliser at the rate of 112g per sq m (4oz per sq yd) and the soil raked to produce a good tilth. Sow the seeds thinly in 1cm (½in) deep drills 30cm (12in) apart. Later thin the seedlings to 23cm (9in) apart in the rows. The plants should be kept well watered and free from weeds. In this respect it helps to put down a moisture-retaining and weed-suppressing mulch of peat to cut out the need to hoe near the roots which bleed easily if damaged.

Pests and diseases

None of any consequence.

Harvesting

In October or November the roots can be lifted with a fork. In mild areas both salsify and scorzonera can be lifted throughout the winter as required. Alternatively the crop can be lifted in the autumn, the top growth twisted off and the roots stored in boxes of peat in a cool, frost-free shed or garage.

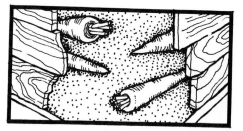

42

Swede

Swedes are a delightful orange coloured root vegetable with a sweet yet peppery taste. In the north of England and Scotland, swedes are served mashed and considered almost a delicacy. The beauty of swedes is that they can be harvested in October or later and so provide a source of vegetables all winter.

Sowing and planting

This must be one of the easiest crops to grow. All you have to do is rake over the soil from which another, different crop has just been harvested. Pull out any weeds at the same time. In cold districts, the seed can be sown in May. However in warmer areas it is better to wait until June or the beginning of July. Sow the seed thinly in drills 1cm ($\frac{1}{2}$m) apart. Leave 38cm (15in) between rows and thin the seedlings to 30cm (12in) apart as soon as they are large enough to handle. If you wish to obtain 'spring greens', leave part of a row unthinned. Keep well watered and free from weeds, either by hoeing or putting down a mulch.

Pests and diseases

Flea beetles, root fly and club root.

Harvesting

Swedes can be lifted from October onwards for use when required. In mild areas the crop can be left in the ground over winter. Elsewhere the roots can be dug in November, the tops twisted off and stored in boxes of moist peat.

Swedes are an extremely hardy winter vegetable.

Swede

Brassica rutabaga (fam. *Cruciferae*)
Biennial grown as an annual
Size Roots are globe-shaped from 8cm to 10cm (3 to 4in) in diameter.
Edible part The root, but swede tops can also be used as 'greens'.
Climate preferred Cool temperate.
Aspect Open.
Sowing to harvest time 20 to 24 weeks.
Yield 5kg (11lb) to a 3m (10ft) row.
Soil Any fertile soil.

Parsnip

The parsnip is a valuable fresh vegetable in winter. Either leave in the soil or store the roots in boxes of peat for use during unfavourable lifting weather. A touch of frost is said to improve flavour.

Parsnip

Pastinaca sativa (fam. *Umbelliferae*)
Hardy biennial grown as an annual
Size 15cm to 30cm (6in to 12in) long by 5cm to 8cm (2in to 3in) in diameter.
Edible part The root.
Climate preferred Cool temperate.
Aspect Open and sunny.
Sowing to harvest time 30 to 34 weeks.
Yield 4kg (9lb) to a 3m (10ft) row.
Soil Deep rich, fairly light soil but most soils with correct varieties are suitable.

The trouble with parsnips is that they require such a long growing period in the soil, but many people will find the wait for that pale yellow sweet-tasting flesh worthwhile. There are three distinct varieties. The short-rooted kinds are the best choice for stony soils or where the parsnip disease, canker, is troublesome. The intermediate varieties are a good choice for general cultivation as they offer top yields combined with first-class flavour. The long-rooted types are superb for the show bench and for gardens with ideal soil conditions, but unless you are prepared to go to a great deal of effort they are best avoided.

Sowing and planting
The soil should be dug deeply in winter. Lime can be added if necessary, but on no account add any organic matter which would cause the parsnip roots to fork. Before sowing break down the soil thoroughly with a fork. Before the soil is raked level a dressing of granular vegetable fertiliser may be applied at the rate of 112g per sq m (4oz per sq yd). Depending on the weather and where you live, the seed should be sown in March or April, in drills 1cm ($\frac{1}{2}$in) deep with 30cm (12in) between them. Place the seeds three to a cluster at 20cm (8in) intervals along the drills and later thin out to leave just one plant at each position. Hoe to keep the soil free from weeds and water when necessary.

Pests and diseases
Aphids, carrot fly, leaf miner and canker (roots rot for which there is no cure, but grow resistant varieties).

Harvesting
The roots are ready for lifting when the foliage dies down in the autumn. Lift as required. The roots can remain in the soil over winter as frost improves the flavour. Alternatively lift a few roots and store in a box of peat for use during unfavourable lifting weather.

Turnip

Turnips come in all shapes and sizes and in various colours from pure white to yellow; there are turnips with purple skins and others with skins of greenish gold.

Sowing and planting

The soil for turnips should be dug over in winter and limed if necessary. Alternatively you can sow in ground from which another, different crop has just been harvested. Before sowing, if the soil is known to be in need of fertiliser it may be dressed with granular vegetable fertiliser at the rate of 56-84g per sq m (2-3oz per sq yd) and raked level. The aim should be to produce a seed bed which is firm and yet has good tilth. This may mean treading the soil before the final raking. Early turnips can be sown in succession from mid April onwards in drills 1cm (½in) deep with 38cm (15in) between the drills. Maincrop turnips can be sown in late July to mid August for harvesting in October for storage over the winter. For 'turnip tops' sow thinly in late August and do not thin out. Early and maincrop seedlings should be thinned initially to 8cm (3in) apart when they have developed their first rough turnip leaves. A couple of weeks later, thin again to leave the turnips 15cm (6in) apart. These thinnings can be used for cooking. Hoe frequently to keep the soil open and free from weeds. Water copiously if the weather is dry.

Pests and diseases

Flea beetles, root fly and club root.

Harvesting

Early varieties should be lifted as you require them. They are at their best when about the size of a tennis ball. In October the maincrop varieties can be lifted with a fork, dried, the tops twisted off and the roots stored in boxes of peat.

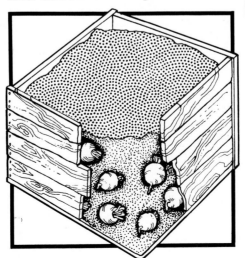

Above Start pulling early turnips as soon as they are large enough to use. If left to age they become coarse and fibrous and are only suitable for making soup. Incidentally, the leaves of the turnip are as good to eat as the roots. Pick the leaves when they are tender and cook like spinach.

Below Lift late varieties of turnip, twist off the tops and store the roots in boxes between layers of peat.

Turnip

Brassica rapa (fam. *Cruciferae*)
Half-hardy biennial grown as an annual
Size Roots are cylindrical, flat or globe-shaped and vary from 5cm to 10cm (2in to 4in) in diameter.
Edible part The root, but turnip tops can be used as 'greens'.
Climate preferred Cool temperate.
Aspect Open.
Sowing to harvest time 7 to 14 weeks.
Yield 4kg (9lb) to a 3m (10ft) row.
Soil Any fertile soil.

Lettuce

Lettuce

Lactuca sativa (fam. *Compositae*)
Perennial grown as an annual
Size 10cm to 30cm high by 10cm
to 20cm wide (4in to 12in by
4in to 8in), depending on the
variety.
Edible part The leaves.
Climate preferred Cool temperate.
Aspect Open and sunny, but in
summer lettuces are better in
partial shade.
Sowing to harvest time 8 to 14
weeks.
Yield 10 to 30 heads, depending
on the variety, to a 3m (10ft) row.
Soil Well drained and rich in
humus.

There are three types of lettuce: cabbage,
cos and loose-leaf lettuce. The cabbage
types in turn can be sub-divided into
'butterheads' with soft, floppy leaves, and
'crisp hearts' which have crisper leaves
than the butterheads and are more
resistant to heat and less liable to run to
seed. Cos lettuces are upright and have
crisp self-folding leaves. They do not run
readily to seed and their leaves remain
much cleaner during spells of torrential
summer rain. Loose-leaf lettuces do not

'heart up'; instead they provide a supply
of lettuce leaves over quite a long period.

Sowing and planting

The soil for lettuces must contain plenty
of organic matter if solid-hearted plants
are to be produced. Two weeks before
sowing or planting out the soil may be
dressed with granular vegetable fertiliser
at the rate of 56g per sq m (2oz per sq yd).
For a summer crop, sow outdoors in
succession from late March to late July

to produce lettuces from June to October. For an early winter crop, sow a forcing variety in August and cover with cloches from September to provide lettuces in November and December. Forcing varieties can also be sown in the greenhouse from August to October to provide lettuces from November to April. For a spring crop outdoors, sow a hardy winter variety at the end of August or in September and harvest in May. For lettuces outdoors in April, sow a forcing variety at the beginning of October and cover with cloches. The seed can be sown thinly in short drills, 1cm (½in) deep and transplanted later to 10cm to 30cm (4in to 12in) apart, depending on the variety. Or you can use pelleted seed and place the individual seeds in the drills 5cm (2in) apart with 10cm to 30cm (4in to 12in) between the rows and later thin out to the required spacing. This method gives faster results as lettuces do not react well to being moved. Another possibility is to raise the plants indoors and to transplant outdoors when they can be handled easily. Avoid overcrowding and water as necessary to prevent bolting.

Pests and diseases
Aphids, birds, millipedes, root aphids, slugs and botrytis (grey mould).

Harvesting
Cut well-hearted lettuces just before they are wanted for use in the kitchen; pick just a few leaves from each plant of loose-leaf sorts as required.

Left *Lettuce can be classified into three groups: the cos lettuce (1), the cabbage lettuce which has a soft round shape (2), and includes the crisp-hearted lettuce (3), and the loose-leaf lettuce from which individual leaves may be picked as required.*

Opposite page *In order to promote firm hearts in cabbage lettuces and to discourage them from bolting, they should be spaced well apart and watered regularly.*

Chicory

Above *Before using chicory, either raw in salad or cooked, the outside leaves should be removed and the stalks trimmed.*

Below *It is neither the root nor the leaf of the chicory plant which is eaten but the blanched shoots produced by forcing, which are called 'chicons'.*

Chicory

Cichorium intybus (fam. *Compositae*)
Perennial grown as an annual
Size The chicons are about 15cm (6in) high.
Edible part The blanched chicons.
Climate preferred Cool temperate.
Aspect Open.
Sowing to harvest time 16 to 18 weeks.
Yield 12 chicon producing roots to a 3m (10ft) row.
Soil Well drained and rich in organic matter.

Chicory is an odd vegetable. For it is grown for neither its leaves nor its roots, but the blanched chicons which are produced by forcing the roots in warmth and darkness.

Sowing and planting

Chicory can be sown on soil which was well fed for a previous crop, or you can dig the plot deeply in spring and enrich it with plenty of garden compost. Dress the area with 175g per sq m (6oz per sq yd) with carbonate of lime, unless the soil is already chalky or limey. Sow the seeds in late April or early May on a prepared seed bed, 1cm (½in) deep in drills 38cm (15in) apart. When the seedlings have three leaves, thin to 23cm (9in) apart. Keep the plants weed-free and well watered.

Forcing and harvesting

In late October or November when the leaves are dying back, lift the roots carefully. Discard any roots which are obviously thin or otherwise imperfect. Good roots are about 5cm (2in) thick at the top and around 25cm (10in) long. Trim back the roots to 20cm (8in) and cut away all the leaves above the crown. Store the roots in a shallow trench in the garden, crown-end uppermost. Only a few roots should be forced at a time to produce chicons. Pack five roots in a 23cm (9in) diameter plastic flower pot containing sand or fairly moist potting compost. Cover with another pot and place in a dark spot where the temperature is 10-13°C (50-55°F). Cut the chicons about an hour before they are required and when they are 13cm to 15cm (5in to 6in) long.

Pests and diseases
Slugs.

Endive

Endive looks just like a curly headed lettuce, but it has less of a bland taste. It is generally in season from late August until early winter and its main advantage is that, being hardier than most lettuces, it provides a very useful contribution to autumn salads.

Sowing and planting

The soil should be prepared by digging in plenty of organic material and dressing with granular vegetable fertiliser at the rate of 56g per sq m (2oz per sq yd) about two weeks before sowing. The seed can be sown thinly at intervals from June to August in drills 1cm ($\frac{1}{2}$in) deep and 30cm (12in) apart. As soon as the seedlings can be handled easily, they should be thinned to 23cm (9in) apart. As endive seedlings do not transplant readily, the thinnings should be discarded. Some people prefer blanched endive to reduce the plant's bitterness. This can be achieved by covering the heads for 14 days with large flower pots to exclude the light. Alternatively the leaves can be tied up together using raffia.

Pests and diseases

Virtually trouble free.

Harvesting

Cut heads as required just before they are wanted for use in the kitchen.

Endive can be blanched by putting a flower pot over the plant once it is nearly fully grown. Inspect the endive from time to time.

Endive

Cichorium endivia (fam. *Compositae*)
Annual
Size 30cm (12in) high.
Edible part The leaves.
Climate preferred Cool temperate.
Aspect Open, but also partial shade and positions facing north and east.
Sowing to harvest time 14 to 20 weeks.
Yield 12 heads to a 3m (10ft) row.
Soil Well drained and rich in humus.

Mustard and cress

1

2

Mustard and cress are usually grown together and used in their seedling stage for salads and sandwiches.

Sowing

Although mustard and cress can be grown outdoors in fine soil rich in organic matter, it is far better to sow the seeds indoors in succession to provide usable quantities of the vegetables as required. Fill small plastic seed trays or flower pots with moist seed compost and scatter the seeds over the top. Cover the containers with newspaper until the seeds germinate. Then place the containers on a sunny window ledge. Keep well watered. The vegetables can be made available all year round by indoor sowings in this way. Outdoors the sowings should be made on fine soil, in the same way, from April to September.

Pests and diseases

Virtually trouble free.

Harvesting

Cut the seedlings with scissors when they are about 5cm (2in) high.

1 Sow the seed evenly over the surface of the compost and make a fairly thick cover of seed.
2 Press the seed into the compost and cover with newspaper until the seeds germinate.

Mustard and cress

Sinapsis alba and *Lepidium sativum* (fam. *Cruciferae*)
Annuals
Size 5cm to 8cm (2in to 3in) high.
Edible parts The seedling leaves and stems.
Climate preferred Cool temperate to sub-tropical.
Aspect Open and sunny (or under glass).
Sowing to harvest time 15 days for mustard, 18 days for cress.
Yield 225g (8oz) from an area 25cm by 25cm (10in by 10in).
Soil type Fine and moisture retentive.

Radish

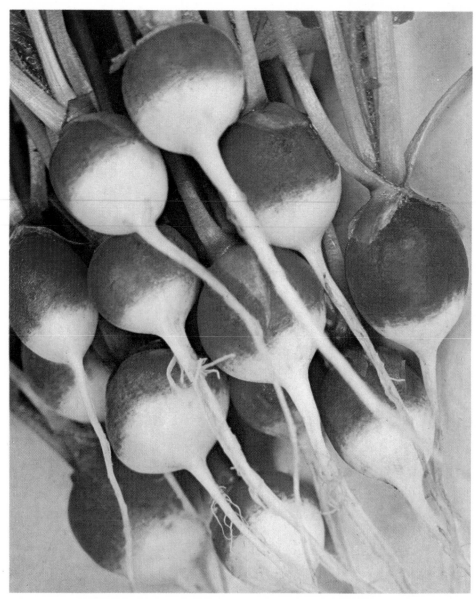

With their mild, peppery flavour and crunchy texture, radishes are a perfect addition to salads.

Radish

Raphanus sativus (fam. *Cruciferae*)
Biennial grown as an annual
Size Roots of summer radishes are round about 2.5cm (1in) in diameter or long and measure 5cm (2in) in length; winter radishes are round 10cm (4in) in diameter or long and measure 20cm (8in) in length.
Edible part The root.
Climate preferred Cool temperate.
Aspect Open.
Sowing to harvest time 4 to 6 weeks, summer varieties; 10 to 12 weeks, winter varieties.
Yield 2kg (4½lb) to a 3m (10ft) row, summer varieties; 4½kg (10lb) to a 3m (10ft) row, winter varieties.
Soil Well drained and rich in humus.

There are a great many varieties of radish of which the most common are the small round radish and the long oval radish. Radishes vary in colour from pink, red and purple through to black and white, and, in shape, from round to long and tapering. The variation in size between different varieties is also quite marked. The flesh of the radish is crisp, white and firm, and has a hot peppery flavour. The leaves of young pink radishes may also be eaten.

Sowing and planting

Unless the soil is rich in organic matter or has been fed for a previous crop, fork in some peat or *well-rotted* compost. Summer varieties should be sown in succession from March to early August in drills 1cm (½in) deep and 15cm (6in) apart. Sow very thinly to cut out the need for thinning. If overcrowding does occur, thin the seedlings to 2.5cm to 5cm (1in to 2in) apart. Winter varieties should be sown from late July to mid August in drills 23cm (9in) apart and later thinned to 15cm (6in) apart. Hoe to keep down weeds and water well in dry spells as fast-growing radishes never recover from drought.

Pests and Diseases

Flea beetles and root fly.

Harvesting

Pull summer varieties from the garden as required while the radishes are still young and tender. Winter varieties can be left in the soil and lifted during the winter as required, but it is better to lift them in late October; remove the loose soil, twist off the top growth and store the roots in boxes of peat in a frost-free cellar, garage or garden shed.

Beetroot

Beetroot is very easy to grow and its sweet fresh flavour is a welcome addition to any salad. As well as the normal dark red beets, there are golden beets and white beets, which, as well as being equally delicious, add colour and interest to the table. This delicious vegetable also has a high nutritional value.

Sowing and planting
The soil should be dug over in winter and peat or well-rotted compost added if necessary to lighten it. About two weeks before sowing the soil may be dressed with granular vegetable fertiliser at the rate of 112g per sq m (4oz per sq yd). Sow the seeds very thinly 2.5cm (1in) deep in rows 30cm (12in) apart. Successional sowings can be made from April to June for a steady supply. The maincrop for winter storage should be sown in early June. As soon as the seedlings can be handled easily, thin out to 5cm (2in) apart. Later thin to 10cm (4in) apart and use the thinnings for salads. Hoe regularly to keep down weeds and water when necessary to prevent the roots from splitting. The maincrop is best mulched with moist peat in summer.

Pests and diseases
Leaf miners.

Harvesting
Lift small beetroots as required. The maincrop should be lifted in early October and the roots dried and any loose soil rubbed off. Twist off the foliage and store the roots in boxes of peat in a frost-free shed or garage.

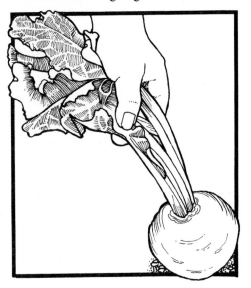

Below *Always lift beetroot by hand and remove the leaves by twisting them off. If the roots are cut they bleed and deteriorate in quality.*

Above *Beets harvested with care will be without blemish.*

Beetroot

Beta vulgaris (fam. *Chenopodiaceae*)
Biennial grown as an annual
Size Roots can be used between 4cm and 8cm (1½in and 3in) in diameter.
Edible part The root. The leaves can also be cooked like spinach.
Climate preferred Cool temperate.
Aspect Open.
Sowing to harvest time 12 to 18 weeks.
Yield 3kg (6½lb) to a 3m (10ft) row, early varieties; 4kg (9lb) to a 3m (10ft) row, maincrop.
Soil Fertile and light. Heavy soils can be made suitable by adding peat or well-rotted compost.

51

Stems and stalks

Celery

Celery produces crisp stalks which are eaten raw in salads from late summer to spring. They are also splendid cooked as a vegetable in soups and stews.

Sowing and planting

There are three types of celery: trench varieties, which provide stems in late autumn and winter, self-blanching varieties which are ready from late summer and which are milder in flavour, and American green celery which is ready for use in summer; this celery has a pronounced 'nutty' flavour. These latter varieties have taken the back-ache out of celery growing. The plot for self-blanching and American green varieties should be dug over in April, adding as much compost or manure as possible.

Trench varieties require a special trench which is also prepared in April, by digging out the soil 30cm (12in) deep and 38cm (15in) wide for a single row of plants, and 45cm (18in) wide for a double row. The trench should then have liberal quantities of compost or manure forked into the soil in the bottom. Some soil removed when the trench was dug should now be returned to it so that the level of the trench is raised to 15cm (6in) from the top of the trench. The remaining soil should be used to make mounds 8cm (3in) high on either side of the trench. In April, sow the seeds in compost indoors and prick off when 1cm (½in) high into boxes of potting compost. Keep the plants growing steadily and transplant outdoors in June or July. With the self-

Celery

Apium graveolens
Hardy biennial grown as an annual
Size 60cm (2ft) high.
Edible part The stalk.
Climate preferred Cool temperate to sub-tropical.
Aspect Open and sunny.
Planting to harvest time 28 to 34 weeks.
Yield 6.5kg (14lb) to a 3m (10ft) row.
Soil Well-drained but moisture-retentive soil.

blanching and green varieties, plant in squares on level ground 23cm (9in) apart each way. With the trench varieties, space the plants 25cm (10in) apart in a single row down the middle of the 38cm (15in) wide trench; if planting a double row in a 45cm (18in) wide trench, space them 30cm (12in) apart with 25cm (10in) between the rows. Do not stagger the rows, as setting the plants in pairs makes them easeier to earth up later. After you have finished planting, flood the trench with water. Two or three times during July and August the plants may be given a dressing of granular vegetable fertiliser at the rate of 56g per sq m (2oz per sq yd). When the trench varieties are 25cm (10in) high, blanching should begin. Tear off any side shoots emanating from the crowns, wrap the stems in newspaper collars, tie loosely and pile the soil in the mounds at the sides of the trench against the collars. In late September complete earthing-up so that only the foliage of the plants is visible.

Pests and diseases
Celery fly (grubs cause brown blisters in the leaves), aphids, leaf miners, slugs and celery leaf spot (brown rusty spots on leaves and stems—spray with Bordeaux powder every two to three weeks).

Harvesting
Lift the self-blanching varieties as you need them. The trench varieties are ready about nine weeks from the start of earthing-up. Remove plants from the end of the row as required, taking care to avoid disturbing neighbouring plants.

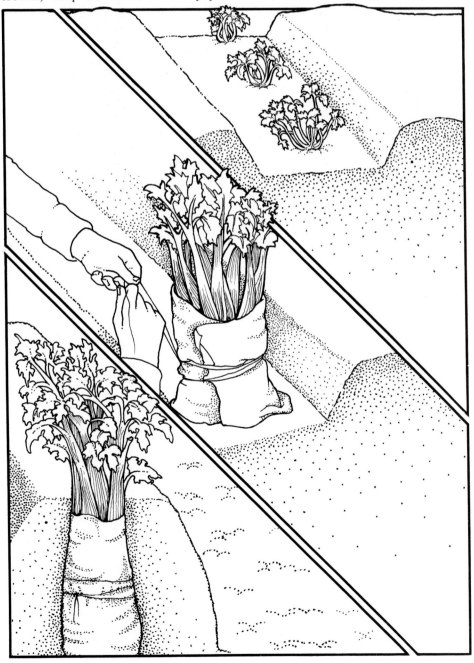

Opposite page, left Celery that has been successfully blanched should have beautiful white, crisp stems.

Opposite page, right Self-blanching celery grown in a concrete frame.

Left Blanched celery should be planted in a trench with equal amounts of soil on either side. When the plant is almost mature, the leaves should be tied loosely together and the whole plant earthed up so that only the foliage of the plants is visible.

Fennel

Above *The delicate ferny leaves of Florence fennel can be used in the same way as those of perennial fennel.*

Below *The bulbous stems of Florence fennel are similar in texture to celery but have a flavour of aniseed.*

Fennel, Florence, or Finocchio

Foeniculum vulgare dulce
(fam. *Umbelliferae*)
Annual
Size 60cm (2ft) high.
Edible part The bulbous stem bases and leaves.
Climate preferred Temperate to sub-tropical.
Aspect Sheltered and sunny.
Sowing to harvest time 20 to 25 weeks.
Yield 2kg to 3kg (4½lb to 6½lb) to a 3m (10ft) row.
Soil Light and sandy preferred, but any well-drained fertile soil gives good results.

The swollen stems of Florence fennel can be eaten raw in salads or cooked to produce a delicious vegetable with a sweet flavour of anise. The leaves of Florence fennel can be used in the same way as those of perennial fennel.

Sowing and planting
The soil should be prepared in winter by digging in some form of organic matter to lighten it and to help it retain moisture in summer. The seeds should be sown in drills 1cm (½in) deep and 45cm (18in) apart. When the seedlings are large enough to handle, thin progressively to 20cm (8in) apart. Keep the plants well watered and free from weeds. As the stems start to swell draw soil up around them to blanch them.

Pests and diseases
Virtually trouble free.

Harvesting
Lift the swollen stem bases when they are about 8cm (3in) in diameter as required in late summer. The surplus crop, can be stored by freezing.

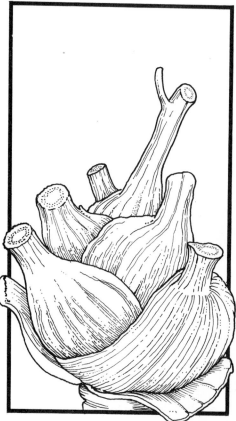

Artichoke, globe

The artichoke is such a decorative plant that it can be grown if desired in a herbaceous border. The edible parts of the plant are one of the greatest pleasures of summer. Raising plants from seed is not recommended because plants do not come true from seed.

Planting
The soil for artichokes should be prepared in winter, by digging plenty of farmyard manure or garden compost, and left in a rough state until planting time. In April fork over the plot and give it a dressing 112g per sq m (4oz per sq yd) of general fertiliser. The plants, obtained from a nurseryman, should be set out 90cm (3ft) apart each way and watered thoroughly. Keep down weeds with your hoe and water well during dry spells. In this respect it helps to put down a 5cm (2in) moisture-retaining and weed-suppressing mulch of compost or peat annually in summer. Each autumn clear away dying leaves and old pieces of stems. In cold districts cover the plants over the winter with straw until the risk of frost has passed. If you wish to produce chards, cut down the foliage of three-year-old plants after harvesting to 30cm (1ft) from the ground to encourage new growth. When the shoots are 60cm (2ft) high, tie them together and blanch them for six weeks with black polythene collars.

Pests and diseases
Virtually trouble free, but leaves can turn brown and plants die back in warm humid weather (artichoke leaf spot). The remedy is to spray with half strength

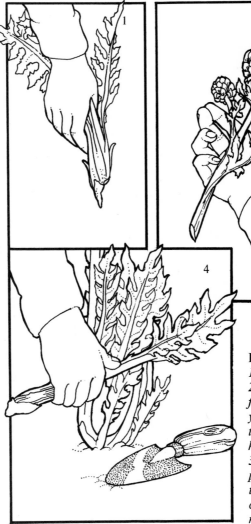

Bordeaux mixture before the heads form.

Harvesting
Cut the heads from late June onwards when they are plump and tender and the scales are tightly closed. The king heads will be ready first. The small side heads can be harvested when they are the size of golf-balls and cooked or eaten raw Italian-style. Once the chards have been harvested, the parent plant should be dug up and discarded.

Propagation
In order to maintain the quality of your artichoke production, it is a good idea to increase and renew some of your stock of plants annually. In April or November, remove the 23cm (9in) long rooted side growths (suckers) and pot them up in 13cm (5in) pots containing potting compost. Suckers taken in November should spend the winter in a frost-free frame or greenhouse and be planted out in mid April. Suckers taken in April should be planted out when a fresh spurt of growth indicates that they are well rooted and firmly established.

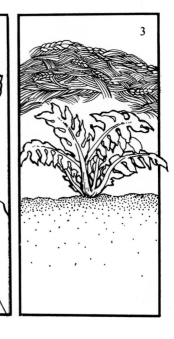

Left
1   Plant offsets in spring.
2   By its second year of growth from an offset, each plant should yield five or more of the large terminal buds known as king heads.
3   In areas susceptible to frosts, protection should be provided for the cut-down plants, such as covering with a layer of straw manure.
4   To propagate artichokes, cut long-rooted side shoots, offsets, from the base of the plant in spring.

Far left *The ornamental thistle-like flower head of the artichoke is as pretty as it is delicious.*

Artichoke, globe
Cynara scolymus (fam. *Compositae*)
Perennial with a useful life of three years
Size 1.5m (5ft) high and 75cm (30in) in diameter.
Edible part Flower buds and the young leaf shoots (known as 'chards' and used like celery).
Climate preferred Temperate to sub-tropical.
Aspect Sheltered and sunny.
Planting to harvest time 17 to 20 weeks from April-planted plants.
Yield Four to six king heads and 10 to 12 side heads per plant.
Soil Well-drained and rich in humus.

Asparagus

For a lot of people asparagus is synonymous with luxury, and the succulent green spears fresh from the garden do have a delicious flavour. It takes years to establish an asparagus bed, but once there, it is a long term asset.

Sowing and planting

In winter dig the soil thoroughly, cover to a depth of 15cm (6in) with well rotted garden compost or farmyard manure and fork this into the soil. If necessary add lime as the soil must be alkaline. Order one-year-old asparagus 'crowns' for delivery in April. These should be set in rows in trenches 15cm (6in) deep and 38cm (15in) apart and covered with 8cm to 10cm (3in to 4in) of soil, leaving the rest of the soil to fill gradually into the trenches over the spring and summer. The second and subsequent trenches should be 60cm (2ft) apart. Keep the bed free from weeds and well watered. In June or July it may be helpful to feed the bed with granular vegetable fertiliser at the rate of 56g per sq m (2oz per sq yd). At the beginning of November cut down the ferns to ground level and top dress the bed with well rotted compost or manure. If you wish to raise asparagus from seed, soak the seed in lukewarm water overnight and sow the seeds in April 1cm ($\frac{1}{2}$in) deep in drills 30cm (1ft) apart on a prepared seed bed. When the seedlings are about 15cm (6in) high, thin to 30cm (12in) apart. Cultivate the plants, as with seakale , from crowns. The following April transplant the young plants to their permanent bed.

Pests and diseases

Asparagus beetles' larvae feed on the foliage and leave the stems bare. The remedy is to spray with derris if you see any greyish grubs. Cut worms eat young roots. Slugs eat shoots.

Harvesting

Do not cut any shoots the first season after planting. In the second season (third from seed) cut no more than one thick shoot from each plant. Using a knife, make the cut 2.5cm (1in) below soil level when the shoots are 8cm to 10cm (3in to 4in) high. In the third season (fourth from seed) cut all the shoots which appear during the first five weeks. In the fourth (fifth from seed) and following seasons cut all the shoots that appear. Using a knife, make a cut 5cm (2in) below the surface when the stems are 10cm (4in) high. Store by freezing.

Asparagus

Asparagus officinalis (fam. *Liliaceae*)

Hardy perennial with useful life of more than 20 years

Size Mature ferns are 90cm (3ft.) high.

Edible part The immature shoots.

Aspect Open, unshaded and if possible on a southerly slope.

Planting to harvest time The plants crop in the second year from crowns, in the third year from seed.

Yield 2kg (4$\frac{1}{2}$lb) to a 3m (10ft) row but increasing with the age of the plants.

Soil Light, sandy and alkaline, but heavy soil is suitable with the addition of compost; good drainage is essential.

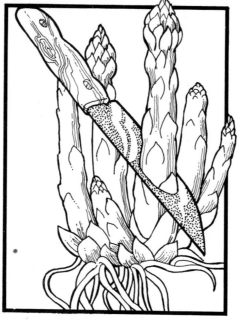

Seakale

Seakale is in season in March and April. The curly green leaves are delicious eaten raw in a salad or cooked like spinach, and the forced young shoots are sweet and succulent.

Sowing and planting

The soil for seakale should be dug deeply and enriched with plenty of well rotted compost. If necessary, lime should be added to make the soil 'neutral'. The easiest way to raise seakale is to plant root cuttings or 'thongs', as they are called, in March. These thongs, flat end uppermost, should be planted so that their tops are 1cm ($\frac{1}{2}$in) beneath the soil surface. Allow 30cm (12in) between each thong and 45cm (18in) between subsequent rows. Generally, you require 15 thongs for an adequate supply of leaves and stems. As the young shoots grow, remove all the weaker ones to leave just one shoot on each root. Remove any flower stems which may form. Hoe to keep down weeds and water copiously in dry spells. If possible, put down a mulch of compost or peat. In October remove the foliage as it dies down. If blanched seakale is not wanted there will be green leaves ready for cutting the following April. To produce blanched seakale, loosen the soil between the rows in January, using a garden fork. Use a hoe to draw up the loosened soil over the crowns of the plants. Where possible spread compost over the crowns so that the soil and compost cover them to a depth of around 25cm (10in). The blanched stems will be ready in April.

A second method of growing seakale is to raise the plants from seed, such as Lily White, sown 2.5cm (1in) deep on the prepared bed in April. When large enough to handle, the plants are transplanted to the same distances apart as a bed produced from thongs. For the first two years, concentrate on building up the strength of the plants for harvesting in the third year.

Pests and diseases

None of any consequence.

Harvesting

The shoots are ready for cutting when they are between 15cm (6in) and 23cm (9in) long. After harvesting allow the plants to grow naturally for the rest of the season.

Propagation

After five years the bed can be renewed by cutting healthy thongs in the autumn from mature roots.

Opposite page, above *Asparagus beds are a long term asset.*

Opposite page, below *To harvest asparagus, gently move the soil away from the base of a shoot and then, using a sharp knife, cut diagonally.*

Above *Seakale growing in its natural seaside habitat.*

Seakale

Crambe maritima (fam. *Cruciferae*)
Hardy herbacious perennial with a useful life of five years
Size 45cm (18in) high.
Edible parts The stems and leaves.
Climate preferred Cool temperate.
Aspect Open.
Planting to harvest time The plants crop in the first year from prepared root sections or 'thongs', but it takes two years to produce a crop from plants raised from seed.
Yield Varies with age, but about 1kg (2lb) per plant.
Soil Well drained and rich in humus.

Vegetable fruits

Marrow, courgette, pumpkin, squash

All marrow and courgette plants have male and female flowers. For fruit to set, the female flower must be pollinated by the male. As this is not always achieved by insects, it is advisable to do this by hand.

Marrow, courgette, pumpkin and squash

Cucurbita pepo ovifera, C. maxima, C. moschata (fam. *Cucurbitaceae*)

Annual

Size Plants of bush types are 90cm (3ft) across; trailing types are 1.8m (6ft) long.

Edible part The fruits.

Climate preferred Temperate to sub-tropical.

Aspect Sheltered and sunny.

Sowing to harvest time 10 to 14 weeks.

Yield Varies enormously with type; but 6kg (13lb) courgettes to a 3m (10ft) row· marrows and squashes yield at least 2kg (4½lb) per plant and pumpkins 2 to 3 fruits per plant, weighing 9 to 14kg (20 to 30lb) each.

Soil Well drained and very rich in organic matter.

The marrow and its relatives provide real fun in vegetable growing providing spectacular results in a relatively short space of time. Marrows come in bush types and trailing kinds, yielding fruit which can be sausage-shaped, oval or almost round. Courgettes are really varieties of marrows which produce small fruits over a long period. Squashes, of which the custard marrow is a good example, are American varieties of the same vegetable. The custard marrow produces a fruit which is roundish and varies from 8cm (3in) to 25cm (10in) in diameter. There are white and yellow skinned forms of this summer squash. Try them in salads or sizzled in butter—they are delicious. Finally there are the pumpkins and thick skinned types called winter squashes which store well. How

about a slice of pumpkin pie?

Sowing and planting

If the members of the marrow family could grow on a compost heap, they would be delighted. That should give you some idea of the amount of organic material you need in the soil. Since most people cannot spare vast quantities of compost or farmyard manure, the solution is to prepare individual compost-filled holes for each plant. Dig out these holes 30cm (1ft) wide and 30cm (1ft) deep 60 cm (2ft) apart for bush types and 1.2m (4ft) apart at least for trailing varieties. Then fill the holes with a mixture of compost or manure and soil. When the risk of frost has passed, generally late May, sow three seeds 2.5cm (1in) deep in each of the filled holes. As soon as the seedlings have two true rough leaves, thin out to leave just one plant in each position. The soil must be kept moist at all times. Water copiously around the plants but not over them. The tips of the main shoots of trailing types should be pinched off when they reach 90cm (3ft) long. Once the fruits start to swell, feed with a liquid general fertiliser every fortnight. Weeds are best

prevented, rather than removed, by putting down a 2.5cm (1in) thick mulch of moist peat. In cold districts plants can be covered with cloches and frames. All plants have male and female flowers. The female flower may be recognized by the embryo fruit behind the flower. The fruit will not set unless the female flower is pollinated. This is not always achieved by insects and hand pollination is often advisable.

Pests and diseases

Capsids (tattered holes in leaves—spray with derris), red spider (leaves marked with pale patches—spray with derris), slugs and botrytis.

Harvesting

Cut courgettes when they are about 10cm (4in) long for use as required; marrows are best when 25cm (10in) long. Constant cutting is essential to prolong fruiting. Marrows, pumpkins and squashes required for winter storage should be allowed to mature on the plants and cut just before the first frosts are expected. Store on slatted shelves or in plastic nets slung between beams in a cool frost-free shed or garage.

Left *A selection of squash.*

Right *Courgettes are only either a special variety of small marrow or ordinary marrows gathered when very young. They should be cut when they are very small. Regular cutting ensures a long-lasting supply.*

Tomato

Originally from South America, the tomato may be red or yellow in colour and round, oval or pear-shaped in appearance. Although botanically a fruit, the tomato is nevertheless treated as a vegetable.

Tomato

Lycopersicum esculentum
(fam. *Solanaceae*)
Perennial grown as an annual
Size 45cm to 1.8m (1½ft to 6ft) high by 30cm (1ft) wide, depending on the type and variety.
Edible part The fruit.
Climate preferred Temperate to sub-tropical.
Aspect Sheltered and sunny.
Sowing to harvest time 18 weeks, greenhouse varieties; 22 weeks, outdoor varieties.
Yield 4kg to 5kg (9lb to 11lb) per plant indoors; 2kg (4½lb) per plant outdoors.
Soil Compost gives best results indoors, outdoors, plants need rich, moisture-retentive soil, or you can use compost in pots or plastic growing bags.

Tomatoes are quite easy to grow, provided that you choose the most suitable varieties for the conditions. Outdoors, bush varieties give the best results in cold districts. They also have the added advantage that they can be covered with cloches to speed the ripening of the fruit.

Sowing and planting

If a heated greenhouse is available (minimum night temperature, 10°C or 50°F) seed can be sown in December to raise plants for setting out in March. However if the greenhouse is unheated, the seed should not be sown until mid March to produce plants for setting out in late April or early May for a July crop. The seed to produce plants for outdoor growing should be sown in late March or early April. At the appropriate time, raise the seeds by sowing two seeds 1cm (½in) deep in peat-based compost in 8cm (3in) wide peat pots. Once the seedlings have their true tomato leaves remove the weaker seedling from each pot. As a temperature of about 17°C (65°F) is required for successful germination in a week to 12 days, the ideal spot for the peat pots initially is a warm cupboard indoors. When the time comes to put the plants in the greenhouse, plant them complete with peat pots in compost-filled growing bags or in 23cm (9in) wide ring pots filled with potting compost and standing on a 15cm (6in) thick aggregate base. It is not a good idea to grow tomatoes in the greenhouse soil as this leads to a build up of soil pests and to diseased plants unless the gardener is willing to replace soil in the greenhouse borders every second year. Tie the main stem loosely to a bamboo cane or wind it loosely up a firmly supported vertical string. Side shoots should be removed when they are 2.5cm (1in) long. Water frequently and start to feed weekly with tomato fertiliser once the first truss of fruit has set. For outdoor tomatoes, the soil should be well prepared by digging in plenty of compost. Otherwise, use compost-filled growing bags or 23cm (9in) plastic pots. Set the plants outdoors in June when they are 15cm (6in) tall, with 45cm (18in) between the plants and 60cm (2ft) between subsequent rows. Standard varieties will require the support of 1.5m (5ft) canes; bush varieties need no support. Watering, feeding and the removal of sideshoots should be carried out as with greenhouse tomatoes, except in the case of bush tomatoes where the removal of sideshoots is unnecessary. With the standard varieties, the tops of the plants should be removed after the fourth truss to encourage all of the crop to ripen.

Pests and diseases

Aphids, white fly (spray underside of leaves with malathion and repeat at seven day intervals), blight (leaves and fruit turn brown—spray with Bordeaux powder from early July), and damping off (seedlings).

Harvesting

Gather the fruit when it is well coloured. Greenhouse tomatoes can be left to ripen on the plants until the first autumn frosts. Outdoor fruit is best picked by late September and the remaining green fruit allowed to ripen indoors in a warm room. Store surplus fruit by freezing.

Red and green peppers

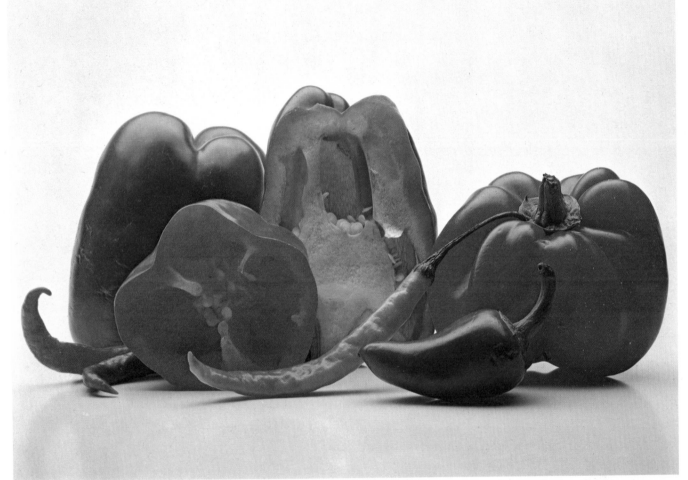

Capsicums, sweet peppers, green peppers and red peppers are all the same vegetable. A red pepper is simply a green pepper which has been left on the plant to mature. Peppers come in various shapes and sizes from the familiar chunky square shape to wrinkled sausage-shapes which are only a mere 6cm (2½in) long. In temperate climes it is advisable, although not always necessary, to grow peppers inside. However, new varieties are being developed which will withstand somewhat colder weather.

Sowing and planting

Sow the seeds in March or April singly, 1cm (½in) deep, in 8cm (3in) wide peat pots, containing peat-based compost, and keep in a temperature indoors as close to 18°C (65°F) as possible. When the plants are 13cm to 15cm (5cm to 6in) tall, pinch out their growing tips to encourage the formation of two leading shoots. If the plants become too large for their peat pots, they can be planted, peat pots included, in 13cm (5in) diameter plastic pots containing peat-based compost. In mid May the plants can be set out, four to a growing bag, in the greenhouse. If you wish to have the plants outdoors, move them to 18cm (7in) wide pots containing a peat-based compost in early June and stand the pots in a sunny sheltered spot. The plants will require stakes. Spray the plants gently with water during the flowering period to encourage fruit to form. Give weak feeds of liquid general fertiliser at fortnightly intervals from the time the fruits first appear until they show colour.

Pests and diseases

Aphids, red spider mites, but generally trouble free.

Harvesting

Peppers are worth picking as soon as they reach about 8cm (3in) in length. Leave the peppers to mature fully if you prefer the sweeter flavour of the red pepper. Store peppers that you cannot use immediately by freezing.

A pepper becomes red or green depending upon how long the fruit is allowed to remain attached to the plant. A red pepper is simply more mature than a green one and has a slightly sweeter taste.

Capsicum, sweet pepper, red and green pepper

Capsicum annum Grossum (fam. *Solanaceae*)

Tender perennial, grown as an annual

Size 50cm (20in) high and 38cm (15in) wide.

Edible part The fruit.

Climate preferred Temperate to sub-tropical.

Aspect Sheltered and sunny.

Sowing to harvest time 13 to 15 weeks.

Yield Depends on variety, but generally 0.7kg to 1kg (1½lb to 2lb) per plant.

Soil Peat-based compost in a growing bag.

Aubergine

Aubergines, sometimes called egg plants, are a good accompaniment to all lamb dishes and are a firm favourite in the United States. Thanks to the introduction of faster ripening varieties, even gardeners without the ideal warm climate can achieve remarkable success in growing them.

Sowing and planting
Sow the seeds in February or March singly, 1cm (½in) deep, in 8cm (3in) wide peat pots, containing peat-based compost, and keep in a temperature indoors as close to 21°C (70°F) as possible. The plants should have their growing tips pinched out when they are 13cm to 15cm (5in to 6in) high to encourage the formation of two leading shoots. If the plants are becoming obviously too large for their pots, they can be planted, in peat pots, in 13cm (5in) diameter plastic pots containing peat-based compost. In mid May the plants can be set out, four to a growing bag, in the greenhouse. If you wish to have the plants outdoors, move them to 18cm (7in) wide pots containing potting compost in early June and stand the pots in a sunny sheltered spot. The plants will require stakes. Remove any side-shoots as they appear and feed with liquid general fertiliser every fortnight. Allow only four fruits to develop on each plant. Regular spraying with water will encourage the fruits to set.

Pests and diseases
Generally trouble free.

Harvesting
Pick the aubergines from late July onwards while the bloom is still on their skins. As the shine disappears, the fruit tends to become bitter. Store the surplus crop by freezing.

Below *The plants should have their growing tips pinched out when they are about 13 to 15cm (5 to 6in) high to encourage the formation of two leading shoots.*

Right *The aubergine is a tropical plant which may also be grown in temperate climes in sheltered areas. Most varieties produce large purple fruit but there are also white varieties.*

Aubergine
Solanum melongena ovigerum
(fam. *Solanaceae*)
Tender annual
Size 60cm (2ft) high and 45cm (18in) wide.
Edible part The fruit.
Climate preferred Temperate tolerated, but mainly sub-tropical.
Aspect Sheltered and sunny.
Sowing to harvest time 22 to 26 weeks.
Yield 4 fruits per plant.
Soil Peat-based compost in a growing bag.

Cucumber

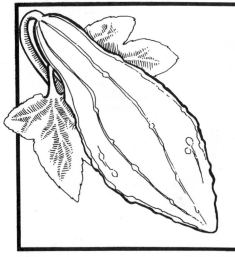

Cucumbers can be divided into basic types: the greenhouse or frame cucumber, with its familiar long fruits, and the ridge cucumber which can be grown out of doors.

Sowing and planting

Varieties for heated greenhouses (minimum temperature 18°C/65°F) can be sown in February. For unheated greenhouses, frames and outdoors, sow in April two seeds 1cm (½in) deep in 8cm (3in) wide peat pots containing peat-based compost. If the pots are stood in a hot, dark cupboard, germination will take place in 4 to 9 days. Once the plants have developed their first true cucumber leaves, thin out to leave one plant in each pot. In mid May the plants for the greenhouse can be set in growing bags or 23cm (9in) wide plastic pots containing peat-based potting compost and trained up a vertical wire or cane. The top should be removed when the plant reaches the desired height. Train the side shoots along wires attached horizontally to the greenhouse glazing bars. The tip of each side shoot should be removed at a point two leaves beyond a female flower. With greenhouse cucumber varieties all male flowers should be removed as fertilised fruit is bitter. Female flowers can be distinguished by the miniature cucumber behind their petals. Keep the soil nicely moist, but not soaking, and feed every two weeks with a liquid general fertiliser after the first fruits swell. Outdoor cucumbers can be grown in compost-filled growing bags or in soil specially prepared for them. Make holes for the plants 30cm wide and 30cm deep (12in by 12in) with 60cm (2ft) between the holes. Then fill the holes with a mixture of well-rotted compost or farmyard manure and soil. A second row of compost-filled

holes should be 90cm (3ft) apart from the first. Such planting holes can be covered in cold districts with frames or cloches. The plants should have their growing points removed when they have seven leaves. Side shoots will then develop and these should be pinched out at four leaves. Once fruit has formed, the fruiting laterals should have their tops removed at a point two leaves beyond the developing cucumber. Keep the soil moist at all times, but water around the plants not over them as this helps to prevent stems and fruit rotting. Feed fortnightly with liquid general fertiliser once the first fruits have formed and support ripening fruits on pieces of tile or board to keep them clean and free from the attention of slugs. Do not remove male flowers as outdoor cucumbers require to be fertilised to produce fruit.

Pests and diseases

Capsids (tattered holes in leaves—spray with derris); red spider (leaves marked with pale patches—spray with derris); slugs (protect plants at planting out time) and botrytis.

Left *Ridge cucumbers fruit prolifically and may be grown out of doors.*

Right *The frame or greenhouse cucumber needs to be grown in humid warmth.*

Cucumber, indoor and outdoor, or ' frame ' and ' ridge '

Cucumis sativus (fam. *Cucurbitaceae*)
Annual
Size 2m (6ft) high, climbing types; 1.2 (4ft) across, trailing kinds.
Edible part The fruit.
Climate preferred Temperate to sub-tropical.
Aspect Sheltered and sunny.
Sowing to harvest time 10 to 12 weeks indoors; 12 to 14 weeks outdoors.
Yield Up to 25 fruits per plant.
Soil Well drained and rich in organic matter outdoors; compost in pots or growing bags indoors.

Index

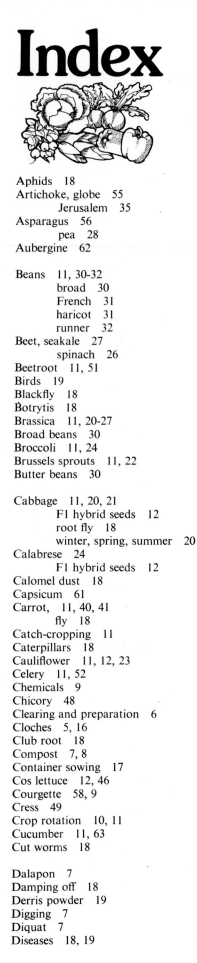